Push Back The Night

*A Clergyman-Columnist's Views on
the Relevance of Religion in the Nineties*

by Milton H. Keene

Nopoly Press, Inc.
Wilmington, Delaware
U.S.A.

First Edition

Manufactured in the United States of America

ISBN 0-930950-39-9 Hardcover
ISBN 0-930950-40-2 Quality Paperback

Library of Congress Cataloging-in-Publication Data

Keene, Milton Henry, 1912-
    Push back the night : a clergyman-columnist's views on the relevance of religion in the nineties / by Milton H. Keene.
        p.   cm.
Includes index.
ISBN 0-930950-39-9 : $18.75 — ISBN 0-930950-40-2 (pbk.) : $12.75
1. Christian life — 1960- 2. Christianity and atheism. I. Title.
BV4501.2.K414   1992
270.8'29 — dc20
                                                    92-20659
                                                      CIP

To my family, who have helped
me push back the night.

Nopoly Press, Inc.
One Wellington Road
Wilmington, Delaware 19803-4129
U.S.A.
302-764-8918

Preface

After writing the newspaper column entitled "Think It Over" for more than thirty years for the Wilmington, Delaware *News Journal,* I proposed to my editor a column with an undisguised religious thrust.

He was interested, but wasn't quite sure what style, form, and content he wanted it to take. Definitely, he didn't want anything "preachy." Neither did I.

Over several weeks I tried a number of approaches, but they didn't quite hit the target — which was a little hard to do anyway, since, as he said, "I don't know what I want, but I'll recognize it when I see it."

So I kept trying. Since the *Journal* is a daily and Sunday newspaper, it was important, it seemed, that the column have something to do with news: names, places, dates, figures — all that sort of thing, dear to the hearts of newspaper people.

I didn't want it to be too serious, yet serious enough to give respect to the news, but with a lighter touch here and there, as seemed desirable.

Finally I hit on it. The right stuff! (At least in the opinion of my editor and his fellow staff members.) "Go ahead" came the message. So, for over two years now, the column has been appearing in the paper.

Some of the subjects are controversial, hence receive a good share of both criticism and approval — depending upon which side of an issue the reader may be on. Most comments are supportive and encouraging. But even the negative ones do me good and make me think. So, thanks to all the readers, writers, and phone callers for their reactions.

These columns, when put together in book form, reflect the times we Americans have lived through during the recent past: good times, bad times, frightening times, challenging times, sad times, glad times, times of war, times of peace — and always, times of change.

If there seem to be inconsistencies in the columns as they appear here, part of this can be charged to the inconsistencies of the times themselves and part to the inconsistencies of my own mind. The latter is ever changing — like the moon, but always orbiting about one central sun: my faith in God, my Maker, and in Jesus Christ, my Lord.

Should anyone perceive a more critical attitude toward current Methodism than toward other contemporary denominations, mark this down to the fact that as a Methodist minister I speak with the gentle criticism of a member of the family. If I seem to speak critically of other denominations, it is in good will and a fraternal desire always to help and never to harm.

Publisher's Foreword

Happily, I have known Milton H. Keene for 43 years and can testify that he is a man of many talents. Writing seems to be one of his best. Therefore, it is a great personal pleasure to me to be able to publish this book. As he indicates, he has been writing for "our" local newspaper (Delaware and nearby counties of Maryland and Pennsylvania) for many years.

There is one feature of his ministry that has to be extremely unusual, I believe: He served three different United Methodist churches which members of my family attended. This started in Wilmington, Delaware in 1949, where I attended. A number of years later, he served my sister Frances in Seaford, DE and — after official retirement — he served my sister Ethel for quite a few years in Cannon, DE.

Milton, in addition to counseling couples about to be married, as I suppose every minister does, has for many years done professional counseling. I believe much of this tended to marriage problems.

I suppose it isn't necessary to say that I like Milton's writing very much. The reasons for that are: First, he selects very interesting and timely topics. Second, his views are presented clearly and colorfully. Third and last, he says a lot in a limited number of words.

As is said elsewhere, the brief chapters in this book have appeared as columns in the Wilmington, DE *News Journal*. In addition, since the *News Journal* is owned by the Gannett Co., publisher of a great many dailies, the column appears in some of those papers as well.

Because the author brings into his writing a large number of persons, publications, and events, it seemed as though the book begged to have an Index. I'm glad this is readily available to you the reader.

Russell W. Willey

Contents

Page

1.   What a Year for Religion!

The year 1989 stood wide-eyed as religious values were punched and pounded, squeezed and stretched, tossed and gyrated like a hunk of dough in Joe's Pizza Parlor.

There were the Bakker, Dortch, and Swaggart imbroglios when the whirling pizza almost spun out the window into a bewildered gaggle of spectators.

Then there was Ted Turner, featured on the cover of *The Humanist,* the magazine put out by The American Humanist Association. The article on the inside pages had Turner telling the world that "Christianity is a religion for losers."

The cable mogul elaborated on the subject by pronouncing the Ten Commandments obsolete. For the enlightenment of the world that had dwelt in darkness before his coming, Turner patronizingly offered ten "Voluntary Initiatives" as a new and improved substitute for the original ten.

Hold on! What's this coming? A request from Soviet Russia asking for—of all things—twenty million Bibles! Close on the heels of the amazing request came the announcement that the erstwhile atheistic nation has officially authorized a study of the Ten Commandments in complete indifference to Turner's decalogue.

Accompanying all this came the shocking confession that Marxism has failed mainly because it lacked the moral fiber to hold things together. So the world's real "losers" are asking for those "obsolete" commandments to help them stop losing.

Meanwhile, in another corner of a very confused year, Vice President Dan Quayle, beating on an old drum, was making a speech about Communism's "hatred of God."

He had scarcely put aside his notes before Mikhail Gorbachev came along confessing that he was a baptized Christian, and that he was packing his bag for a visit with Pope John Paul II in the Vatican.

Gorbachev acknowledged that the Soviets have done an about-face in their attitude toward religion, "which, admittedly, we used to treat in a simplistic manner."

Jesus took something of a trouncing in 1989. So what's new? He's always been a good target for the fool-makers who end up making fools of themselves.

Martin Scorsese's "The Last Temptation of Christ," which did a broad-brush job on the human nature of the man from Nazareth, took liberties with Jesus' good, hard-won reputation by representing him as a confused, pathetic, guilt-ridden figure, more in need of salvation than offering it.

Then, with the artist's flair for creativity at all costs, Andres Serrano offered to the world an "art" photograph of a crucifix immersed in the artist-photographer's own freely-given urine specimen, bearing an outhouse title.

But, for better or worse, we just can't seem to get Jesus of Nazareth off our minds. He has captured our imagination, and survived the barbs and arrows, the clown-robe crown and scepter forced on him by those earlier clownmakers. What were their names? And who will remember Serrano's name two thousand years from now?

By the way, a recent Gallup Poll revealed something interesting — after two thousand years. Two out of three people, offered the choice of eight historical personalities they would like to spend a day with, said Jesus.

And the tough world of politics and economics is feeling the impact of his influence. Whether they realized it or not — and many of them did — the students demonstrating peacefully in China's Tianamin Square were marching to the beat of his drum.

The beat came through Martin Luther King who heard it in Mahatma Gandhi, who heard it in Leo Tolstoy, the great Russian novelist, who heard it echoing in the words of Jesus in the New Testament.

And the events which toppled the Berlin Wall picked up the

Galilean beat—through Lech Walesa in Poland, and hundreds of churches in Leipzig and Prague and other cities of Eastern Europe.

Dan Rather on "CBS Evening News," reporting from Prague, kicked off a week of reports called "God and Gorbachev." Tom Bettag, the Evening News executive producer, explained why he had launched the series: "There's a major religious revival at work here, and it's undermining Communism."

What a year for religion! And this is not the half of it.

2.   Religion's High Ground

As the 90s came roaring in, full throttle and volume up, it was a good time for Americans to consider the rights we claim — and the wrongs they're laying on us.

The right to be born, and the right to prevent being born. The right to die, and the right to hasten dying. The right to love, and the right to hate. The right to kill, and the right to save. The right to revere, and the right to profane. The right to be a man, and the right to be a woman. The right to believe, and the right to doubt.

In this confusion, people stepping into a new decade bravely attempted to make their way.

Traditionally, it has been the role of religion to blaze trails through the wilderness of difficult decisions and hard choices. But what happens when religion gets caught up in the choices and becomes part of the problem?

The beginning of the 90s found religious groups and individuals glaring at each other from opposite sides of vital issues such as abortion, euthanasia, homosexuality, and war and peace.

Biblical texts were stretched and skewed to serve the purpose of whichever group was making its point, while shouting down the opposition.

Is there no way that religion can find its own higher ground, so that it might lead confused souls through the moral morass of these times? Isn't there some redeeming truth in our sacred texts that will help human beings become less bellicose, more kindly, more of a mind to try to understand another point of view?

Most people I know would agree that there is a high vista from which mankind can view the world with its complicated issues and wearisome conflicts.

In the Christian Bible, which has echoes of its great words and ideas in other sacred scriptures, an idea emerges from the misty flats of human thought, a mountain peak lifting its head above the marshes. The idea leaps into bold, beautiful words in a letter by Paul, the apostle, to a group of early followers of "the Way," living in Corinth on the Greek peninsula.

"If I speak in the tongues of men and of angels, but have not love, I am a noisy gong or a clanging cymbal . . . Love is patient and kind . . . not jealous or boastful . . . not arrogant or rude . . . does not insist on its own way . . . does not rejoice at wrong, but rejoices in the right . . . Love never ends . . ."

Like a man who can't let something great slip from his mind, he brings it up again: "The whole law is fulfilled in one word . . . love . . ." He seems to be telling the world that if you have love in your heart for your fellow human beings, you don't need a law to tell you not to kill them, mug them, rape them, steal from them, or lie about them.

He invites people to walk through the horrendous issues of their times with that kind of love within them and see how different everything looks. Let them shed their arrogance, suspicion, loveless indifference — those old worn-out threads — and put on the better clothes of love, then go out into the world.

They'll still have some of their opinions, but the sharp edges will be blunted, and they may even find themselves ready to consider something that may never have crossed their minds in the old days — the possibility that they could be wrong.

Will religion be a significant force in the 90s, or will it become marginalized — pushed off the edge of the page where significant things are happening? The answer lies hidden in the leaves of the calendar, beginning with January 1, 1991.

If it holds to the low ground of petty party strife and bickering, it will fade into the background and fall off the edge.

But if it rediscovers its own high ground, it can well be the greatest force in human affairs in the 90s and beyond.

Love of life in all its forms and conditions — all its stages and ages — could well be religion's and life's best guide through the confusion which grabs at our hearts and heads as we enter the new decade.

3. The Biggest Story of the Millenium

Bill Moyers, known world-wide as TV journalist and former aide to President Lyndon Johnson, announced some time ago: "I've given up the beat of politics. I've given up the beat of international affairs, because I want to cover the biggest story of the millenium."

Addressing an audience of public relations professionals, Moyers continued, "I'm talking about something far below the surface, a spiritual quest for a new and deeper understanding. . . of faith and what it means to our common life on our planet."

This return to the "religion beat" is an acknowledgement of the unexpressed need of many modern people. People who may or may not find satisfaction in any of the pre-packaged brands of religion offered for public consumption. People who may have rebelled against the religion of their forebears for some reason, but who sense that there's more to life than what money can buy.

The modern world is bored sick by a jaundiced view of life that poses as "reality." The perception of what is "real" is not enough to keep life interesting, much less stimulating.

Kids grow up in a world of slick glossy cars, designer clothes, TV comedy with laugh soundtracks to cue them in on what's supposed to be funny, a world where greed and ego reign in business and politics, and where family life is sacrificed on the altar of greater purchasing power.

"Is this all there is to life?" They sense there ought to be more. And for a while they think it's more of the same thing: more money, more cars, more clothes.

We have torn ourselves from the religious sanctions and sanctities of sex, and we have AIDS. We've lost the religious meaning of work, and we have industrial boredom and product mediocrity. We've divorced ourselves from the religious context of public service, and we have an ethics crisis in government. We've walked out on the religious ambiance of life, and life has become as cheap as last week's newspaper.

Moyers is right. The big story for the next fifty years may well be religion.

If you ever doubted it, take a look at what's happening in eastern and central Europe. If all you see there is political and economic, look again. Look beneath the surface, as Bill Moyers says.

The media has been overflowing with commentary and analysis. News cameras have been flashing atop the crumbling Berlin Wall. Hopeful talk about NATO troop withdrawals. Nervous talk about German reunification. Currency transfers. But this is not the whole story.

As an editorial in *The Christian Science Monitor* points out, "It was in the churches, in the realm of religious ideas . . . that upheaval began."

The first dissenting voices in Poland, back in 1980, were voices made strong by the sanction of the Catholic Church. "In Romania, the courage to face the bullets in Timisoara came from an obscure Hungarian minister named Laslo Tokes."

Throughout the Soviet block, pastors were encouraged by thoughts of Vaclev Havel in his book of essays, *Living in Truth.* Havel, according to his U.S. ambassador, Rita Klimova, is an unorthodox believer.

Some of the strongest opposition in East Germany, before the fall of the Berlin Wall, came from the churches: Nikolai Church in Leipzig, Gethsemane Church in Berlin. These churches have long been havens for protest — for peace, ecology, and democracy.

The so-called "New Forum" opposition groups — all 16 of them — were headed by clergy. Men like Markkus Meckel, a founding member of the GDR Social Democrats, is a pastor. Wolfram Ullmann, head of Democracy Now, is a theological historian. Reiner Epplemann, the dissident head of the

Democratic Awakening, is a pastor.

If from where we stand we see the amazing happenings in eastern and central Europe only in economic and political terms, we're missing the engine that drives them — the spirit of religion, embraced in profound seriousness that is willing to put everything on the line.

4.   Spiritual Is In!

How important is God to us Americans? On a scale of 1-10 where would you rate concern about our relationship with the Ultimate?

Include all those frenetically pressing matters that people talk about whenever and wherever they meet — jobs, advancement, money, cars, houses, community, marriage, family, international relations, peace, war — the whole thing.

If you guessed that God and religion might rate about 1 — at the bottom of the list — you'd be right — right, that is, in the thinking of a few people who profess faith in God on Sunday morning, but have strong doubts about its practical importance in the lives of real people in the real world.

But wrong so far as the facts are concerned. You'll no doubt be as shocked as those other people who seem to think America is more secular than it really is — more focused on greed and get-ahead, and success at all costs than it is upon God and prayer and spiritual forces.

Starting at the bottom of the scale in a survey of 600 adults conducted from January 17 to 20 of 1991, only a low 2% of those asked said that a good-paying job is the most important thing in their lives.

Health rates higher up the scale along with a happy marriage, but guess where one's relationship to God is. Try 2 instead of 1 or maybe 4, or better still, try 5. If you can adjust to the rarified atmosphere, try 7. If you're not completely overcome yet, try an 8, or — are you ready for this? Try 10.

A score of 10 for faith in God? Unbelievable! Impossible!

Unrealistic! Absurd! But wait a second before you disbelieve yourself off the edge of reality.

The reality — or so the survey by Princeton Survey Research Associates reveals — is that for 40% of those questioned, their relationship with God is the most important part of their lives.

Those who had us Americans pegged as materialistic, secular, or ungodly are just plain flabbergasted. "An astounding set of figures," says Wade Clark Roof, a professor of religion and society at the University of California in Santa Barbara. "It suggests a re-orientation, a cultural shift."

But is it a temporary shift, a flash-in-the-pan reaction to the Gulf War, the economic downturn, or perhaps the fall from lofty economic heights of heroes like Michael Milken and Donald Trump?

No doubt these enter into the current mood of Americans and the new orbit of interest around spiritual values. But it's not temporary, say outstanding sociologists like Robert Bellah of Berkeley and Martin Marty of the University of Chicago School of Theology. Marty says, "I think that people are going to look back at today as a hinge period in the country's history . . . Spiritual is in."

Does all this hungering and thirsting after spiritual things add up to a pie-in-the-sky philosophy — an escape from the concerns of this world through wild flights of spiritual fancy? Hardly. Along with the new spiritual hunger for God, there is a renewed interest in one's fellow man and improving the human condition here on earth.

One of the tests of genuine spirituality is whether or not one's relationship to God turns the spiritual seeker toward his fellow man in his human need. Applying this test, the present mood of many Americans seems truly, genuinely spiritual.

At the root of the American shift from "greed is good" is a disenchantment with the Yuppy philosophy, a realization that there's more to life than money can buy.

Marsha Bristow Bostick of Columbus quit a job that paid her $150,000 a year, saying, "I found myself wondering how wealthy do we need to be? I don't care if I have a great car, or if people are impressed with what I'm doing for a living."

Stuart Winby, a manager at Hewlett-Packard, discussing the

brash secularism of the 80s, says, "Those kinds of values are just empty. I'm sated with gadgets, things, adornments, and all that stuff." (*TIME* magazine, April 8, 1991)

In these contemporary statements there are echoes of other, more ancient, words: "A man's life consisteth not in the abundance of things which he possesseth."

5.　　　　We Can Do Better

Have you ever noticed how irritable, even downright mean, some religious folks get when their religious sensibilities are stepped on? They reach a boiling point fast, and almost (if not completely) lose their religion in defending it.

In earlier times "good Christians" have burned other "good Christians" at the stake for holding and expressing views contrary to their own.

We don't go that far in our modern world — although Salmon Rushdie is still under death threat for publishing his book, *Satanic Verses*, which offends some followers of Islam.

Our western ways of showing outrage are less violent. Instead of burning at the stake, we condemn, ban, and boycott. The milder ones among us simply sit and grouse and commiserate with one another about "how awful" things are.

I'm aware of the series of cheap shots that some of the artistic ilk have recently taken at things sacred, and I confess my dander has shot up at times, and I feel like firing a letter off to somebody somewhere, and just plain yell and stomp and holler.

But we can do better than that, can't we?

Take that offensive bit of "art" created by artist-photographer, Andres Serrano, showing the crucifix immersed in a flask of the artist's urine. To compound the offense there's the irritating fact that American tax money has been used by the National Endowment for the Arts to promote exhibits of the piece.

Outrageous! Irreverent! Obscene! And hooray for ol' Jesse Helms and his call for a ban on federal funding of art that is "obscene."

But we can do better than that. Take the obscenity and convert it. Conversion has always been the lifeblood of Christianity. Before its conversion, the cross itself was a symbol of shame — and was meant to be.

So, since the offense exists, why not dare to look at it and see what the artist himself may never have intended and would no doubt be shocked out of his slimy mind to have discovered.

Serrano's scandalized cross says things that slipped by Serrano in his preposterous attempt to lampoon the sacred symbol — like the fact that the man of the cross in fact descended into the dregs of human existence for human redemption.

Submerge him in the excrement of the world, and there among outcasts, the waste of society, the true glory of the man is seen. If the artist took time to meditate upon the meaning of his work, he might hear a voice speaking through his subconscious, "Look long at what you count worthless in yourself; I will meet you there."

Another event which has disturbed the saints: In Pasadena, Texas, public school officials have scrutinized a peace symbol being exhibited by students, and have detected something "satanic." The symbol is an inverted letter "Y" embraced by a circle.

According to their interpretation, the inverted Y is a cross with its arms dangling helplessly as though in defeat, signaling the failure of Christianity. Hence, a "satanic" anti-Christian symbol.

Now we can do better than that. Let's suppose it's all the bad things the school authorities say it is. Then let them do a very simple thing — turn the symbol over so that the "Y" is upright. Now, if it's a cross at all, it's a cross with arms flexed in an upward sweep — a flying cross, no less. Within the circle it might suggest to devout minds a Winged Victory, reaching out to the farthest expanses of the universe.

Burn, ban, boycott, condemn — these are the historic and modern reactions to offended religious sensibilities. We can do better than that!

One thing certain, Christians, Muslims, or whatever, don't have to be driven to some desperate, paranoid, and vengeful corner when their dearest faith is thrown out with the slop by sick minds.

A sense of humor, a pinch of consecrated imagination, and an ample measure of "good will toward men" could do a better job.

6. Religion Can Be Just Plain Laughable

Take Norman Lear, the playwright. Is he also a: blasphemer, iconoclast, new convert, or just a spiritually-haunted human, hooked by religion he can't get out of his head, and so tries to write it out?

The reason for this scrutiny is Lear's new TV show, "Sunday Dinner," aired for the first time one Sunday evening on CBS.

Donald Wildmon, who sleuths for evil wherever it can be found, and manages to find it almost everywhere — announced the show's debut with typical handwringing in his magazine, *Journal of the American Family Association,* June 1991 issue.

Detecting what he seems to consider heaven-shaking abominations in some of Lear's earlier TV productions, Wildmon quakes at the thought of awful things to come on Sunday evenings as the American soul is put under the CAT scan of the playwright's penetrating humor.

Instead of falling into some fatal funk and pitying themselves for being attacked and embarrassed by the humor, why can't religious folk join in the fun and use it as a catharsis to get rid of some ideas and attitudes which cling to traditional religion like barnacles on a boat's bottom?

Everything that looks and sounds religious is not necessarily that, and everything that looks and sounds irreligious may not be irreligious.

As a matter of fact — and history — some of the most religious-sounding things are enemies of true religion. And some of the most irreligious-sounding things are truly religious.

"Mr. Lear," says Wildmon, ". . . has ridiculed and demeaned Christians and Christianity in past television programs," such as "All In the Family" and "Mary Hartman, Mary Hartman."

Wildmon recalls such theologically poignant moments as when Archie Bunker pontificates upon the divine nature: "Of course God never makes a mistake; that's why he's God," declares Archie with a note of finality meant to end all debate on the subject.

Was Lear demeaning Christianity through the blusterings and bombast of Archie Bunker, or was he demeaning what deserves demeaning—an attitude easily discerned among some people who arrogantly posture and pose as knowing all there is to know about God?

When Lear had Archie launch his profound statement, he was playfully knocking the heads of people whose depth of understanding of the spiritual goes no deeper than something they learned in some Sunday School under the tutelage of a teacher who had hurriedly scanned the lesson material while sipping his or her last cup of Sunday morning coffee.

Like many other well-intentioned but misinformed people, Archie was a zealous defender of the faith as he misunderstood it. He would fight for what he misbelieved at the drop of a word. Take for example the episode in "All In the Family" when everybody in the family was discussing the baptism of Archie's new grandson.

The parents were not in favor of it, but Archie, good traditionalist that he was, favored it, and proposed that the baby be baptized whether Gloria and Meathead wanted it or not. When Edith opposed him, Archie's righteous temper flared, and he demanded, "You gotta use force; that is the Christian way."

To Archie it was an urgent matter involving the eternal salvation of his grandson. Christianity, as he misunderstood it, taught that if the child should become ill and die before baptism, he would be eternally lost—damned. So it was of slight consequence to Archie whether his attitude alienated the parents, Edith, and everybody else, he was righteously intent upon forcing the thing through.

From clips like these, some people conclude that Lear is a blasphemer, speaking of holy things in unholy ways, laughing at the sacred. But instead of condemning the honest mirror that the playwright holds up to the unattractive face of society, why not condemn the ugliness of society which the mirror reflects?

Is Lear an iconoclast, an image breaker? He is — and with humorous vengeance, because he sees many images that should be dashed to make room for what is better than the image.

In an episode of "Mary Hartman, Mary Hartman," he has the Rev. Jimmy Joe, an eight-year-old evangelist whose father is exploiting him to get rich, fall into the bathtub with his radio while listening to the 6:30 news and is electrocuted.

Loretta, one of the characters in the play, sincere but not too bright, who has absorbed bits and pieces of the Christian faith and strung them together in a bizarre necklace, said about Jimmy Joe, "He died for the 6:30 news, for the sins of the 6:30 news."

It's laughable, and Lear intended it to be. But it's also pathetic, demonstrating how people pick up various religious concepts and create some hodge-podge theology out of them, and proclaim it as the eternal gospel.

Some things can best be addressed and attacked through humor — as dueling was dismissed from civilized practice, not by frontal attack, but by laughing it out of existence.

More than he may realize — yet perhaps not more than he might ardently hope — Lear may be laughing certain irreverent, simplistic, even stupid, religious ideas off stage so that the stage can be cleared for better things in religion.

7. Rush to Judgment

"Waddaya think of this guy Jim Bakker?" a friend asked me.

"Frankly," I said, "my thoughts are a mixed bag."

"Mixed?" He had the look of a man who expected something "better" from me, some spurt of hot volcanic invective.

If he had asked me earlier when the news first broke, I might have given him exactly what he wanted.

When I heard about the pay-off and the cover-up of his affair with Jessica Hahn, I was outraged. Then with the news of the skimming operation, charging him with pocketing more than four million dollars from pledges wheedled from trusting followers, I was just plain mad.

This charlatan had defiled the holy ground he stood on. He had left a dirty smudge on the banner of a sacred calling. He had cheated believing souls who thought they heard in his voice echoes of the Galilean who blessed mankind.

Something in me instinctively loathed this wolf in sheep's clothing who had stolen into the Good Shepherd's fold and ravaged the flock.

Then somewhere between wanting to see him jailed for life and tarred and feathered and strung up by his thumbs, I was stopped suddenly in my inquisitorial tracks by a thought. Or was it a memory of words heard long ago and far away? "Let him who is without sin cast the first stone." Words hurled by Jesus of Nazareth at a frenzied lynching mob with stones ready to pelt the life out of a young woman taken in adultery.

"Give me a break! These words have nothing to do with this situation." I argued with the gentle memory. "This liar, this cheat, this adulterer ought to get what's coming to him!"

But the words were infiltrating my moral indignation, eroding my resolve, mellowing my savage righteousness. Other words from somewhere beyond my maniacal thirst for the blood of the offender came swimming into my consciousness: "The sin of one man reveals the sin in the heart of every man."

Suddenly my righteous ego was impaled on this spear point of truth, left there kicking and thrashing helplessly. The stone, meant for another sinner, dropped from my hand.

I remembered something from Jean Jacques Rousseau's *Confessions:* "Such as I was I have declared myself to be; sometimes vile and despicable . . . Even as thou hast read my inmost soul, Power Eternal, assemble round thy throne an innumerable throng of my fellow mortals. Let them listen to my confessions, let them blush at my depravity, let them tremble at my sufferings, let them each in turn expose with equal sincerity the failings and the wanderings of his heart and, if he dare, aver, 'I was better than that man!'"

My thoughts were going too far — or were they getting too close? Too close for righteous indignation, too close to qualify me for participation in a lynching party?

Something in me would like to stand ensconced in self-righteousness and pray as a Pharisee once prayed in the temple, "I thank Thee, God, that I am not as other men are!" But something else nudges me to sidle over to where a despised publican is praying, "God be merciful to me, a sinner!"

As I told my friend, my thoughts about Jim Bakker are a mixed bag. But when I shake the bag now, what comes to the top of the mixture is the realization that at heart I am no better than that man. All that coaxed, cajoled, and spurred him to his downfall is part of my own human nature, and the makeup of every other human being.

Sex, greed, the longing for success — all fueled and driven by ego — these are inescapable elements of the human constitution.

Like a good novel such as Hawthorne's *The Scarlet Letter*, this inglorious episode in the life of a TV evangelist is a mirror held up before the soul of every man in which he sees not another, but himself.

The law must do what the law must do — and I find no fault in the dispensation of justice. But after considerable reflection, I find myself totally disqualified to withhold mercy from a recreant fallen brother man.

8.   Sin Is an Ego Trip

Are 10% to 25% of American clergy sheep among wolves or wolves among sheep?

Maybe some of both. And part of something else.

Never before in history has the spotlight of public scrutiny fallen more mercilessly upon men of "the cloth." Which means that never before has the clergy been more urgently obliged to justify itself.

Ministry and Sexuality is the title of a newly published book. The author, G. Lloyd Rediger, a Presbyterian minister and confidential clergy counselor with nineteen years experience, claims that about 10% of this country's clergy have been, or are presently engaged in sexual misconduct. Another 15%, says Rediger, are on the verge.

The most recent shocker features Archbishop Eugene

Marino of Atlanta who resigned his post because of a two-year intimate liaison with Vicki Long, an attractive young woman lay minister.

Could it be that the ordained representatives of God are so naive about the powerful currents of male and female relationships that they don't know what's happening until they're swept over the falls?

This is possible. Some theological seminaries offer courses in theology and parish administration and worship, but offer next to nothing to prepare a young minister to deal with the dynamics of sex.

So, in the clergy debacle over sexual malfeasance, we can mark down a point for clergy naivete.

But this isn't all of the story. There's an ego factor in the equation. Sex in itself is powerful enough for most people to handle, but when it's driven by ego, it can become too much.

King David learned this when he became erotically involved with a beautiful young woman whose name was Bathsheba. She was the wife of one of the king's soldiers, Uriah, whom the king sent to "the front," where he was conveniently killed in action.

The wild rationale that raged through the king's brain went something like this: "Why should this lovely creature belong to an ordinary soldier? She's fit for a king! And who's king around here? Me!"

But what has egotism to do with the clergy? Everything.

The most "modest" clergyman — if he is honest enough to face his own soul — will confess that he wants to be the center of attention. He may profess humility, but in the final analysis it's a humility he's proud of.

He is set apart by ordination. This means he's different. That difference could translate into "more important."

Whether it's sanctified by ordination or unsanctified, ego is ego, and it makes its claims.

Why should this lovely creature, Vicki Long, belong to a lesser man and not to him? So might the archbishop reason.

On the woman's part (There is also such a thing as the female ego!) comes the question: "Why should I have a mere man when I can make the archbishop?"

American clergy — Protestant and Catholic alike — are part

sheep among wolves and part wolves among sheep — and part something else called ego.

Rediger's book includes suggestions for developing a clergy sexual ethic, strategies for prevention and support, and "practical guidelines" for avoiding difficulties. One of these guidelines is, "Be as visible and caring as possible. Secrecy and unexplained private events can be dangerous."

Clergy groups, when they meet and discuss fine points of theology and how to increase attendance at Sunday morning worship and a miscellany of other topics, urgently need to discuss the powerful implications of those words in the ancient book of Genesis: "God created man in his own image, in the image of God created he him, male and female created he them."

So, back to the baptismal font or pool for the clergy. Back to a new baptism of honesty and realism in handling God's great gift of human sexuality.

9.   Fleecing the Flock

In the beginning there was Jim Bakker. Then came Jimmy Swaggart. After that, "The Last Temptation of Christ." Next came *Satanic Verses.* And just when the pew-rattling, mosque-shaking sequence seemed over, Madonna's "Like a Prayer" breathed its sensuous images through the sacred precincts of the saints.

And now it's a game called "Fleece the Flock," the irreverent creation of a trio of the more-or-less faithful themselves — Elizabeth Fuller, a Unitarian, Stanley Mason, and Roy Doty, two United Methodists.

"Fleece the Flock." That's the name of the game. What's it all about? You might guess! It's about certain TV "shepherds" fleecing the sheep of their bulging sheep folds, and at the same time attempting to bankrupt and thoroughly ruin fellow "shepherds" who are in the same fleecing business.

The board game which sells for 25 dollars will no doubt bring cynical guffaws from those who "sit in the seat of the scornful" —

if they aren't guffawed out already from the sordid facts which gave rise to the game. And it may offer some comic relief for some people who are still religious and still have a sense of humor.

"In no way is it against religion," says Elizabeth Fuller of Weston, Connecticut, who dreamed up the idea. "It's a . . . game that pokes fun at the TV evangelists who have been taking advantage of innocent people."

And it does that with a vengeance!

Let's say you're sitting down to play the game the first time. To begin, you get 50 million dollars (play money, of course). Right away, you have the feeling of a big entrepreneur in the fleecing business — like Jim Bakker and Jimmy Swaggart and Oral Roberts used to be before their sheep got wise to them and began baaing them out of the sheep pen.

Then you get a miniature collection plate — an important piece of equipment in the fleecing business — to move about the game board, following directions on the cards. Marked "Angel," "devil," and "God's will," cards will either help you or retard your growth toward the goal of the big-time operator.

Some of the messages on the cards might make you blush — if you are still blushable after reading of the actual exploits of some of these characters with whom you're identified in the game.

You pick up a card and read it. "Church secretary seen with you in hot tub." This is called "emergency baptism." Your church officials (remember you're a minister!) are irate over your "baptismal" relationship with the secretary. Consequently, you have to pay each of the other players (fellow TV evangelists, remember) $200,000.

Not a real great start. But you try again with another card. It reminds you that your pious joy is in "saving" bad women. Your brother evangelist, Brother Clem, the card informs you, is saving you a couple for Saturday night. You collect $100,000 from each player.

Another card informs you that your preaching convinces a chimpanzee, by the name of Koko, that there's nothing to the idea that he's in any way related to you. So you get an "Angel" card for your effort.

You're making out like a bandit! But the next card gets you. It seems that the gold nugget ring which you are wearing (a symbol of your success in fleecing the flock) nicks the head of a parishioner you are in the process of healing of some other ills. So you have to fork up $150,000 in damages.

So that's the way the game goes. And all the while you are laughing at the shenanigans of the "pious" brethren, including yourself in the TV evangelist role.

Except for your awareness of the disenchantment of people who have been fleeced, not for "the Lord," but for some ego-centered, fast-talking, money-grabbing empire builder, living in a million dollar home, at the expense of trusting, believing "sheep," many of them widows living on Social Security, the game can be funny — in a sad sort of way.

Apparently it's getting considerable publicity. This naturally encourages its creators, and perhaps will in time give them the good feeling of lots of money coming in — the sort of feeling the big-name, big-bucks TV sheep fleecers once experienced before the poor dumb sheep got smart.

As Ms Fuller put it so graciously, "People have had it with these hucksters."

10. Bad Things Shouldn't Happen to Good People—But They Do!

When Dave Dravecky dropped on the pitcher's mound on August 15, 1987, like a man struck by a sniper's bullet, Roger Craig, the Giants' manager, cried. When I heard about it, I felt like crying. So did a lot of other people from coast to coast.

It's not that I'm a San Francisco Giants fan, or even what you'd call an honest-to-goodness baseball fan. In fact, I didn't know I was a Dave Dravecky fan until I read about his comeback from cancer in his pitching arm — through faith and prayer and dogged persistence.

Against all the odds, including Dr. George Muschler's professional judgment, after performing surgery removing fifty percent of an indispensable pitching muscle in his left arm, that his pitching career was over, Dravecky, a devout Christian, made it back through a power always close to him, his faith in God.

With a packed cheering section of people who like to see faith pay off, I was happy to learn of Dravecky's sparkling victory over Cincinnati and to hear of his 3-1 lead over the Expos in the sixth inning.

That young man had opened up doors of hope for thousands of people who believe they can "make it" with faith in God in their corner. People with cancer and other crippling ailments throughout the country were beginning to hope again.

Then, just as he was throwing a fast ball by Tim Raines of the Expos, it happened: The infield heard the sound when Dravecky's femur fractured and he collapsed. The ball bounced pitifully wide of home plate.

When his teammates and others rushed to him, he said, "I think I broke my arm, but I'm not sure. Lord, take care of me."

The prayer was as natural a part of the man as his arm. Like breathing out and breathing in. Thursday night in the hospital, still in intense pain, he was praying with some of his teammates who had come to visit him.

"That's what hurts," somebody said. "He believed so much, then he was let down."

To think he believed so sincerely, tried so hard, and hoped so much — then to have it all collapse like he collapsed out there on the mound. Roger Craig said, "I've never seen a man go down like that. It's unfair."

Terry Kennedy, the Giants' catcher, slammed his mask to the ground. Trying to hold back tears, he said words that must have been muttered under similar circumstances ten thousand times and more: "Bad things shouldn't happen to good people."

The theme is as old as the book of Job, which narrates the experiences of another good man who believed in God, yet suffered the agonies of the damned.

In his book *When Bad Things Happen To Good People*, Harold Kushner, a New York rabbi, raised the question. The rabbi lived with the question for fourteen years before he attempted to answer it. That was after his young son, Aaron, died from an incurable disease, progeria.

The rabbi's "answer" was ultimately not an answer as much as it was a response: "I think of Aaron and all that his life taught me, and I realize how much I have lost and how much I have gained. Yesterday seems less painful, and I am not afraid of tomorrow."

His faith was sharply tested, but he didn't lose it. Job's faith was severely tried, but he didn't lose it. And the odds are against Dave Dravecky losing his — whether his arm recovers or not.

How come? The answer seems to be that people of faith don't hang their faith on a single peg. Faith to them is a response to life — whether it seems fair or unfair, happy or sad, uphill or downhill. They believe in God, not simply because they think things will go better for them — though often they do — but because for them nothing has meaning without faith.

Rabbi Kushner, a wiser, more kindly human being because of his love for his son Aaron, goes on living and preaching faith.

And the chances are that Dave Dravecky, however things turn out for him, will live and die a man of faith for the simple reason that it is only through faith that life and death have meaning worthy of the human adventure.

11.   Yes, Madalyn, There Is a God

Hundreds of Muscovites were waiting in line at a book fair in Moscow. To celebrate the occasion, American atheist, Madalyn O'Hair, was present.

How fitting, even serendipitous, this happy confluence of time and circumstance. A famous atheist among atheists on atheism's home turf.

These people, nourished at the bountiful breast of atheism from earliest childhood, would naturally be expected to recognize and lionize this lady who had successfully driven God out of the public schools of God-fearing America.

Madalyn, the God-killer, here where it all started. Soviet citizens queued up and waiting seemed quite proper, yes, even downright right.

It must have come as more than a mild shock on the famous

lady's personal seismograph that none of the waiting lines was facing in her direction. And what was outright unforgiveable, no one as much as noticed her.

The excitement focused on a counter that was doing a brisk business. Thinking it must be a new book on her favorite theme, significant enough to eclipse her, she made an end run around the crowd for a look.

The dear lady, afflicted with difficulty in believing in anything beyond herself, may have had trouble believing her own eyes. Bibles!

These people packed in by the hundreds were waiting to buy Bibles! What in the world could be happening to the world when a dedicated honest-to-godless atheist of her peerless prominence could be so rudely ignored by Russian people going after Bibles like kids after ice cream cones in August!

One might imagine a conversation between Mrs. O'Hair and an English-speaking Muscovite:

"Have you people completely lost your minds?" she demands, gazing fiercely into the dark eyes of a young man standing next to her. "You people who paved the way for freedom from religion, standing here waiting in line for Bibles!"

"Yes, Madam," the young man replies, smiling. "We did lose our minds about seventy years ago, and ever since we've been scrambling around trying to find them."

The long line begins to move, and they shuffle ahead a few steps.

"I hope you don't think you can find them in this line."

"As a matter of fact, yes we do, Madam. You see, we've been force-fed Marxism all our lives. I have friends who have been jailed for practicing Christianity. I have witnessed the closing of thousands of churches. But thank God, things are changing.

"I thought you people in America were fully informed about everything. I'm surprised you haven't heard that there's a religious revival happening here — right in these streets where Lenin and Stalin thought they had buried the last traces of faith in God."

Her face reddening at the sound of the word that is a malediction in her lexicon, Mrs. O'Hair listens as the young man continues. He tells her, among other things, that the Russian

Orthodox Church is asking her own America and other western nations for millions of Bibles.

"And you may be interested, Madam, to learn that the Soviets have authorized a study of the Ten Commandments."

"Why, for pity sake?"

"Because the government is reaching for a value system to replace the one that has failed."

"You mean atheism?" Madalyn sizzles.

"Yes, Madam. It has certainly failed. We're interested in something that works, and atheism doesn't work."

"Well it works for me," rejoins Mrs. O'Hair loftily.

"It works for you, dear lady, because you are like a flea living on a dog. Without the warm body of faith in God that exists in your country, you could not survive."

12.   When Atheists Beg for the Bible

"Get this," I said to a friend recently, "they're asking for 20 million Bibles in Russia."

"What do they want any Bibles for? They're atheists. Atheists don't read the Bible."

"They're not all atheists," I said. "According to this clipping from Religious News Service, there are sixty to a hundred million Christians there."

"You're foolin'."

"No — it's the gospel truth."

"Yeah, well, I guess they ought to have Bibles if they want them — livin' among all those atheists."

That's when I zapped him with this: "It's not just Christians who want the Good Book. Atheists want it too. Here it says that a Bishop Vladimir of the Russian Orthodox Church claims he's never talked with a non-believer in Russia who doesn't want a Bible. Says every family in the country wants one."

"I don't get it; but if that many people really want a Bible that much, well, I've got half-a-dozen or so tucked away in desk drawers and chests and other places. They're good as new, gilt edges and all. Got 'em for perfect Sunday School attendance or somethin'. They can have them. I don't use them."

"Wrong language," I said.

"Huh? Oh yeah."

With this he launched himself into a sentimental reminiscence of his personal familiarity with the Bible. "We had one in our house when I was just a kid. Family Bible I think they called it. Great big book. Only time we brought it out was when Mom heard the preacher was comin'. Then she would dust it off and put in on the marble-top table in the parlor—that's what we used to call the front room. The parlor and the Bible got dusted off together."

While he was droning on, I was wondering why the Russians were pressing so hard for copies of the Sacred Scriptures. The request was made by several Russian Orthodox leaders in talks with Terje Hartberg, a publishing consultant with the United Bible Societies.

As Hartberg listened, he learned that the demand "would not even slow down" until there were at least twenty million Bibles in Russia. At the time there were only three to four million.

Later, I looked for an answer in Glasnost, the parting of the Iron Curtain and all that. Maybe better relations between USA and USSR. None of these seemed to be the reason. Furthermore, the need had been expressed long before these changes in the international weather.

Then I turned to Solzhenitsyn, Russia's prophet in exile, author of *The Gulag Archipelago*, who had served time in Russia's labor camps for criticizing Stalin. After being awarded the Nobel Prize for literature in 1970, he was expelled from USSR in 1974.

Maybe this man could throw some light on the subject. In an interview published in *TIME* magazine, I found the answer. "For 70 years," Solzhenitsyn said in reply to a question, "we have been destroying everything in our country, the life of the people, its biological, ecological, and moral and economic bases. Naturally people look to the past for some point of support, some constructive idea."

Some point of support. The Bible, of course! A wind blows through those pages, a spirit close to the hungering and thirsting of the human spirit. There's a feeling of "more," an eternal plus beyond the daily grind. And there's a courage breathing through the pages. Ordinary men with strange fire in their eyes daring to stand before kings and tell them they were wrong.

And in the midst of it all, that one solitary figure who, for many, represents the fairest of our human flowering. Jesus of Nazareth, offering mankind a power and glory that lift them out of frustration and despair, giving them undying hope.

The Bible, of course!

13.   A Candle in the Darkest Night

The sneer is off the face of Soviet atheism. Wiped away by reality. Seventy years of it — gone with its contempt for "weaker" souls who needed to believe that, above the state, the party, and five-year plans, there was something the human mind hungers and thirsts for. Something that we call God.

Recently the Soviet legislature ended years of trying to blow out the candle of faith in the Russian soul. By a vote of 341-1 the government was forbidden funding of atheist propaganda.

Henceforth, according to the verbiage of the legislation, the Soviet government will not "restrict the study, financing, or propagandizing" of religion.

This opens the gates of religious freedom to fifty million Muslims, thirty million Russian Orthodox, six million Catholics, two million Jews, one million Baptists — and thousands more who are not recorded in any religious count.

"Opiate of the masses" they called it. A drug to help the less sophisticated and less intelligent to make it through the days. Weaker people who needed to believe that there is a mind greater than the human mind, a power greater than human power.

One thing they overlooked is that human beings are "incurably religious." Religion is not the creation of priests and prelates. It is the response of the human psyche to the overwhelming evidence of reality—that there is far more to this universe than any one of us or any group of us can explain or take credit for.

More than this, there is something in our human makeup which craves some kind of relationship with the mystery that embraces all things.

On even a deeper level, there is a feeling of incompleteness in us which reaches out for completion beyond all human and material relationships.

Furthermore, there is a dignity that comes with faith in God which enhances work and productivity and supports community and national life.

In 1931, thousands of Muscovites looked on in silent awe and outrage when, under orders of Joseph Stalin, the largest church in the land, the Church of Christ the Savior, was demolished.

Where the beautiful church with its five domes was blown up, Stalin planned to erect the Palace of Soviets, to be crowned with a giant statue of Lenin, symbolizing the victory of atheistic Communism over Orthodox Christianity.

But Stalin's palace or victory was never built. An atheist victory is not proclaimed today in the streets of Moscow.

There has been a turnabout in Russia. In fact, the most popular celebration in 1988 was not a commemoration of the victories of atheism, but a celebration of 1,000 years of the Christianity which Stalin attempted to wipe out. A millenium ago — in 988 — Prince Vladimir of Kiev introduced Orthodox Christianity into his domain.

As James H. Billington wrote in the *Smithsonian* magazine, "Rediscovering the beauty of the Christian past plays a cleansing role for many in Mikhail Gorbachev's Russia. Restoring the old seems almost to be a kind of moral prerequisite for moving on to something new."

Instead of driving religion out of the land along the Volga and beyond, repression and persecution seem to have driven it in deeper.

As one who himself has participated in the persecution put it, "Religion is like a nail. The harder you hit it, the deeper it goes into the wood."

And religion is deep in the wood of Russia. Among its

thinkers of the past are Nikolai Berdyaev and Leo Tolstoy. It was Tolstoy who, through his writings on the life of Jesus, influenced Mahatma Gandhi. And it was Gandhi who influenced Martin Luther King. And it was King who influenced the students in China's Tianamin Square.

The sneer on the face of atheism in Russia has changed to a mask of sadness, even penitence. One more gargoyle in the temple of mankind's faith in God.

14.   A Nation Repents

Evangelist Billy Graham, who was in the Soviet Union before the failed coup, talked with Boris Yeltsin and Mikhail Gorbachev personally about their views on religion.

Both men agreed that there is a desperate need in Soviet society for three things: "some philosophy, some religion, (and) an inner strength."

These words sound strange from the mouths of two men who presided over what for seventy years had been touted as a nation which discounted faith in God, and any morality, philosophy, or social system which in any way reflected such a faith.

Remembering Krushchev's taunting threat about burying us, it would be easy to gloat over the failure of the Communist system. But gloating is never a mature response to others' misfortune. In addition to being immature, it leads to pride, one of the seven deadly sins.

The Soviets had their pride, which sang to the tune of shoe-banging Nikita Krushchev. For us, or any other nation to do no better than that would be at least unbecoming and at most plain stupid.

Instead we can use what's happening in the former Soviet Union as a lesson in humility and repentance. For the leaders of a great nation to confess that for seventy years they have been wrong is no small penitential act.

And for them to reject their historic leaders who for decades have been national heroes is comparable to Americans marching on Washington and dynamiting the Washington Monument. Then, still on righteous rampage, gathering at the Lincoln Memorial and pulling down the pensive figure of the great emancipator, leaving it a heap of fragmented stone.

What's happening in Russia is nothing less than national repentance, the kind that the reluctant prophet, Jonah, sought for the city of Ninevah, to save it from self-destruction.

There have been few more dramatic demonstrations of national contrition in world history than what is occurring in the land of Lenin and Stalin, Krushchev, Brezhnev and company.

A recent ABC-TV show linked Mikhail Gorbachev and Boris Yeltsin with live audiences in a number of American cities. In response to a question put to them by a Philadelphia minister, both men said things that would have heaped hot coals of condemnation upon them just a few years ago.

Gorbachev said he respects the feelings and religious beliefs of all citizens and has worked to guarantee their religious freedom. From Yeltsin came the assurance that he also respects believers and makes "a point of attending church ... quite often, because during the service there's a kind of internal feeling of moral cleansing."

This quote from *National and International Religion Report* of September 23, 1991, is a far cry from the old Communist canard, "religion is the opiate of the people."

Allowing for political "conversions" on the part of these men in response to the ground swell of religious renewal throughout Russia and the other republics of the Soviet Union, their statements reflect the thinking of many people in eastern Europe, and may well reveal their own.

According to *TIME* magazine of September 9, 1991, "White House planners are anticipating a reemergence of Christianity in Russia, bringing with it a moral framework that has long been absent from Soviet political life."

This ought to give pause to all nations, including the United States, who, while never having officially turned their backs on faith in God, may not have made as much of the faith as they might have.

This also raises the question: Now that we can no longer

scorn Russia as a godless nation, and pride ourselves —
sometimes less than justifiably — as a righteous, godly nation,
what will we do with the faith which once seemed to glitter so
grandly against that "dark, godless night"?

15.　　　The Prosperity Gospel

Some of the religious ideas coming at you by way of TV may
sound different from what you're accustomed to hearing. That's
because they are different. Purposely different. Different by
design.

This is pointed out in a book recently published under the
title *The Agony of Deceit.*

After searching publications and sermon tapes, the twelve
contributors, including former U.S. Surgeon General C. Everett
Koop, who sounds off on faith healing in one of the chapters,
have discovered that some TV preachers are saying some rather
strange things in the name of religion.

The book zeros in on a few greats of the television pulpit —
some spared in earlier exposes. Robert Schuller of "The Hour of
Power" and Pat Robertson of "The 700 Club" are caught in the
act of skewing the Christian doctrine of original sin.

Schuller, the book points out, says "the core of sin is a lack of
self-esteem." This may be true in some stretched-out sense, and
the notion may have strong appeal for many of the followers of
the Crystal Cathedral preacher.

But, if the idea sounds more like it was fished out of some
popular do-it-yourself book than drawn from the Bible, it may be
so.

Explaining this apparent divorce of preaching from its
biblical roots, one of Schuller's aides says Schuller believes in the
doctrine of original sin, but that he tries to adapt biblical
principles to the modern audience. "The gospel . . . has what
every human being is looking for," explains the aide. "The
problem is that we're not marketing it."

This makes good sense — up to a point. Transmitting the "old,

old story" to new generations and new mind-sets has always been a challenge, and the challenge has often been grandly met through the years by men and women who have made honest efforts to speak the old truths in a new language.

But in doing so, they were always aware of the dangers of trying so hard to accommodate the original message to contemporary audiences that the original message was lost in the process.

The Agony of Deceit comes down pretty hard on preachers like Paul Crouch of the Trinity Broadcasting Network, Robert Tilton and Kenneth Copeland — all of whom seem to have made a fatal leap into the sin of hubris, or pride — a leap easily made from Schuller's springboard of self-esteem.

Paul Crouch declares that we human beings have the right to claim, "I am a little god." Tilton preaches that "man was designed or created by God to be the god of this world." Copeland, running close in this god-bent pursuit, says, "You don't have a god in you. You are one!"

The real bell-ringer in the little god chorus is Kenneth Hagin of Tulsa, Oklahoma, who edifies his followers by telling them, "You are as much an incarnation (of God) as . . . Jesus of Nazareth." To this amazing declaration he adds the observation that Jesus himself needed to be born again.

Oral Roberts, in the book, gets the dubious credit for being the pioneer who blazed the trail for "the prosperity gospel" —with its promises of blessings for contributions to his ministry.

But, as might be expected, others, even more brash in their approach and more generous in their promises (backed by God, of course), came running down the sawdust trail.

Robert Tilton, based in Texas, persuades his followers to believe that God is bound to give them whatever they "claim" through faith.

"That's right!" he says. "You can actually tell God what you would like his part in the covenant to be!"

Tilton suggests these steps in drawing up a covenant with God: First, let God know what you need from Him. New car. New job. Fitness. House. Finances. Salvation.

After letting God know what his responsibilities are, the viewer makes his "best gift" to God — preferably a contribution to the Tilton ministry.

Following this, God and the Rev. Mr. Tilton "decree the miracle into existence in the name of Jesus."

The editor of *The Agony of Deceit,* Michael Horton, according to a story in *TIME* magazine, says that too many Evangelical clergy and lay people are ignorant of basic Christian doctrine, and so they are easily misled by slick preachers who "sling the right lingo" and emphasize emotional appeals over rational thought.

16.   Prayer and Reality

Can you believe what congregations of believers are praying for these days as they gather in worship? Such things as AIDS . . . divorce . . . substance abuse . . . miscarriage . . .

If they're not praying for these things, they soon will be, according to Anita Manning, writing for *USA TODAY.*

For example, the United Methodist Church is publishing a book of prayers in 1992. Believe it or not, the book will include a prayer dealing with the emotional trauma associated with miscarriage.

The prayer, written by the Rev. Karen B. Westerfield Tucker following her own miscarriage, will raise many eyebrows, if and when it gets by the editors' pens. It has already encountered controversy.

Andy Langford, editor of the Book of Worship, says if you have a miscarriage service, you're going to run up against the moot question about when life begins. The service will imply that life begins with conception, and a miscarriage is the loss of a human life; hence, mourning is a reasonable, heart-felt response.

The service as written affirms this: "Lord, we do not understand why this life, which we had hoped to bring into this world, has been taken from us. We only know that where there was sweet expectation, now there is bitter disappointment."

The prayer cuts through all biological and political opinions — as true prayer does — and asserts that life is life, whatever stage it has reached, and to lose it is great loss.

Prayer doesn't wait for congressional approval or scientific assessment. It rises from the heart and lifts its appeal to life's Source, God.

Prayers for the sick have always been in order — ever since Jesus went about healing the blind, the palsied, the halt, and the lame.

But prayers for people stricken with AIDS! Isn't this going just a little too far for a congregation of worshippers on a clear, bright, sunlit holy day?

Some will argue that such a prayer will be a wink of approval toward any and all human behavior which may be responsible for the condition.

But again, the prayer will push through all other considerations to the victim, the human being, with his or her thoughts and feelings.

Then there's substance abuse. All kinds of attitudes — judgmental, critical, cynical — crowd around the issue like ants at a picnic. A prayer for this!

Yes, the new Prayer Book will offer these words, in the presence of the person or persons involved: "Give strength to (the persons named) . . . bound by the chains of addiction . . . Restore to them the assurance of your unfailing mercy and strengthen them in the work of recovery."

Gone is the condemnation, the social reproach — lifted through prayer to God, who alone knows the human heart. For a moment all mouths are shut, all voices silenced — except prayer, the voice which reconciles all the disparities and angularities of life in the mercy of God.

And what about divorce, long a tabooed subject where people of faith gather? To pray to God for people going through the throes of divorce could be considered a tacit acceptance of the institution and a pious assertion that it's okay with God.

But the prayer moves through all judgmental thoughts and words to the heart of the matter — two human beings who are hurt, lonely, disappointed, angry, bitter, resentful.

The prayer gathers up all these feelings in the words: "We have tried but have failed. We ask that you forgive our weakness. We pray for those who have been hurt by our failure. Lead them and us to forgiveness."

Methodists are not alone in obliging their prayers to wrestle with the problems of today. Catholics are doing the same. So are the faithful of Judaism.

It seems that life, to be meaningful, must be keyed to the great rhythms of prayer. And prayer, to be significant, must be in tune with life where it is lived and where it is most real.

17.   **Prostituting the Bible**

"It's right in the Bible!" The face was white, turning red with anger. The language was Afrikaans but it might have been English or any other tongue.

The place was South Africa, though it could have been America. The individual was an Africaner, one of the million white members of the Dutch Reformed Church, though he could have been a Methodist, Baptist, Presbyterian, or whatever from Delaware, Maryland, or Virginia.

The point of heat was Apartheid, but it could have been any subject where lines are drawn between individuals, and one asserts that he's better than the other, superior in intelligence, nobler, worthier.

The speaker was doing his self-righteous best to vindicate Apartheid in South Africa, as the Dutch Reformed Church there has argued for years — that the institutional injustice is justified in the sight of God, "It's right here in the Bible!"

This kind of argument from "the revealed Word of God" came to a screeching halt recently when 330 delegates from 70 denominations, including leaders of the Reformed Church, issued a ringing statement.

"We confess our own sin and acknowledge our heretical part in the policy of Apartheid, which had led to such extreme suffering," the statement declared. "We denounce Apartheid in its intention, its implementation, and its consequences as an evil policy."

While the statement did not single out any one denomination

by name, it confessed that all South African churches should have done more to resist the vicious institution.

"Some of us actively misused the Bible to justify Apartheid, leading many to believe that it had the sanction of God," the statement continued.

Misuse of the Bible! A painfully disturbing phrase to come from a convention of churchmen — disturbing to all Bible-believing people throughout the world.

Some present at the gathering wanted to soften the phrase by saying that they had not consciously misused the Bible to justify the South African policy of discrimination. They confessed that they had been guilty of supporting the philosophy that the Bible is concerned only in individual salvation and cares nothing about social transformation and change.

While this happened in South Africa, its effects may well reach into every pulpit and congregation throughout the world. The words are sharp and have a point to them.

Wherever there's a Bible and a preacher preaching from its words, wherever there are people who read the most popular book ever published, and give copies of it to their children and grandchildren at Christmas time, there will be a silent challenge in its pages not to misuse the great words and ideas to justify "man's inhumanity to man" or make human beings less human.

I've listened to people who are sincerely convinced that they are Bible-believing people, justifying their bigotry, even malice, by saying, "It's right here in the Bible!"

For years the institution of slavery was justified by slave owners by citing certain passages from the Bible. And for generations, Christians have justified their prejudice against Jews by claiming, "It's right here in the Bible!"

Also there's a long inglorious history of witch burnings and the torching of heretics by people who claimed they were "just following the Bible."

From South Africa to America, to every little hamlet and village, every city and metropolis, it's time to call a halt to the misuse of the Bible for purposes of prejudice, bigotry, and greed.

If the sacred book has one clear message echoing through its pages, it is this: There is a loving God seeking to reconcile the world to himself and human beings to one another.

The message from South Africa is that it's time to challenge all wild-eyed Bible thumpers and wavers as they declare, "It's right here in the Bible, friends!"

18.   Trivialized Religion

"What are you giving up for Lent?"

"Candy. I think I'll give up those delicious chocolate-coated peanut clusters that I love almost as much as life itself."

"How about you?"

"You know me. Sundaes and sodas. Leave the whipped cream off the apple pie — that sort of thing."

This conversation might have occurred any place in the Western world since Ash Wednesday ushered in the season called Lent.

Every season of the sacred calendar is fair game for this kind of frippery and trivialization. That which we don't know how to deal with on serious terms, we trivialize.

With Advent, it's "Do you have your Christmas shopping done yet?"

With Christmas, it's the Christmas tree and toys and turkey.

With Easter, it's Easter bunnies and baskets and egg dyeing.

All innocent enough but trifling, thereby fastening attention on what is inconsequential and keeping it from what is vital.

Lent, since the Middle Ages, has been a season of penitence and confession of sins. It marks the forty days Jesus spent in the wilderness of Judea, tempted by the devil, and it forebodes his impending rejection by the Jerusalem authorities. All of this in a season meant to focus upon sin and forgiveness.

But, since we find it difficult and embarrassing to face our sins and make honest confession, we trivialize them.

A study by Roman Catholic bishops, investigating the drop in the traditional confession, concludes that the decline is the result of "a less pervasive sense of sin." Parish priests say that the reason is "general confusion over what is right or wrong."

Catholic laity say there is another reason — what they call "reconciliation experienced by other means."

A less pervasive sense of sin could be a result of not taking sin seriously, making light of it, trivializing it, joking about it.

General confusion over what is right or wrong can be caused by the same thing. Treat everything with the light touch of whim and frivolity, and nothing is to be taken seriously — including human life.

"Reconciliation experienced by other means" may be a reference to our present tendency to relieve guilty persons of their guilt through medications, support groups, and certain forms of counseling.

The end result is to lift the "mea culpa" from human shoulders and replace it with a kind of no-fault insurance.

Adultery used to be a sin. Today it is called "sex addiction." This is a condition for which an adulterer or adultress is not responsible in the old sense of being accountable for one's sins.

For a fee of $16,000 Patrick Carnes, a Minnesota psychologist, promises to "cure" the problem at his Sexual Dependency Unit.

Some time ago, Karl Menninger of the Menninger Clinic in Kansas, wrote a book titled *Whatever Happened To Sin?* This was an outstanding psychiatrist's inquiry into the trivialization of a condition once taken seriously.

The modern medical approach to human behavior may be responsible in part for the trivialization. *If everybody who was once considered a responsible violator of the moral law is now considered "sick," there is no longer any question of right and wrong, only sick and well.*

Herbert Fingarette, an addiction expert at the University of California at Santa Barbara, says that the "disease model" sends harmful messages to abusers. It excuses irresponsibility, and indoctrinates people with the idea that they're helpless and sick.

We trivialize sex. We trivialize honesty and loyalty. We trivialize the difference between right and wrong. It is frighteningly possible that, if we continue down this road, we'll trivialize the human race out of existence!

19. God Is Not Embarrassed To Be Called Father

Fatherhood is making a comeback — and none too soon! Somehow the house has seemed empty without dear old dad. When was it that we began to think we could do without him, that he was a kind of throwaway plastic cup, no longer important once he had fulfilled the procreative function?

First we reduced him to a buffoon, a bumbling, inept, awkward character who was laughed off the stage. Wanting to play the "good sport," dad cooperated with the act, even throwing in some gratuitous goofs and gaffs to prove he could not only take it, but that he was big enough to join in the fun.

When we want to get rid of something objectionable in our social system, we first make fun of it. Which raises the question, what was it in the fatherhood role that disturbed us so much that we wanted to get rid of it?

Was it the paternal role of disciplinarian, law giver, preserver of law and order in the family, establisher of limitations, punisher for violations?

Let's face it — we don't really like the firm hand, the meting out of comeuppance. We prefer the freedom to do whatever we want whenever we want to do it. Limitations, admonitions, commandments, retributions — they're just not our cup of tea.

So goodbye father! Hello freedom! Ring the bells and blast the sirens on a new age. The new morality was here.

It's not a coincidence that with the farewell to fatherhood, there was a farewell to God — to God at least as Father. In the name of excluding sexist language from the Bible and other religious texts, there have been attempts to dilute the concept of God. This was bound to happen, since thinking of God as Father may tend to elevate the paternal role to the divine level.

The revision of *The United Methodist Hymnal* came under the scrutiny of those dedicated to remove what were termed sexist references to God. One feminist-inspired move that was rejected by the committee proposed the inclusion of a new hymn titled "Strong Mother God."

After years of living with a diminished fatherhood and its consequences, it seems we're ready to reinstate the disciplinary role of fatherhood and welcome back the God who is not afraid to say "Thou shalt not . . ."

Among the first hints that fatherhood is making a comeback was the Oscar-winning film "On Golden Pond" in which Henry and Jane Fonda drew back the curtain on the tensions and longings for reconciliation between a woman and her father.

One of the hottest themes in Hollywood, according to a report in *USA Today,* is parent-child reunions. It's not surprising that the vehicle used in portraying the reconciliations is comedy, since it was comedy which drummed the retreat of fatherhood.

In "Indiana Jones and the Last Crusade," Harrison Ford as Indy and Sean Connery as his dad, who have not spoken to each other in twenty years, are shown tied together back-to-back in a flaming Nazi fortress. Together — literally — they figure out how to outsmart their Nazi captors — driving home, you might say, the point that father and son need each other in a mixed-up world.

Reconciling to dad is the theme of the comedy "Parenting," directed by Ron Howard. In the picture Steve Martin, as a conscientious father, is determined to prove that he is a better dad than his own dad. Gradually, through the agonies of paternal reality, he comes to an appreciation of what it means to be a father, and so he sees his dad in a more sympathetic light.

In the movie "Dad," Jack Lemmon plays an elderly man whose self-centered son, played by Ted Danson, is reconciled to his father in the wake of a family crisis.

So, whether by the back or front door, through comedy or serious drama, father is coming home, and perhaps also the God who, we can believe, is not embarrassed to be called "Our Father . . ."

20. The Baptism of Evil

Remember the days when you could get a clergyman to pronounce a blessing and offer a prayer for anything from a new sewer line to a world war?

Those were the days when church and state cozied up to

each other, and presented a united front of "God and country," this despite the church-state separation clause in the Bill of Rights.

It was a strong force, uniting diverse segments of the citizenry. Whatever represented the flag and the cross or the star of David struck a pose that seemed invincible.

During World War I, women gathered in churches and folded bandages and knit sweaters for "the boys over there." Preachers chopped texts from the Bible to throw on the fires of patriotic zeal. Young men were lauded in local congregations for their "greater-love-hath-no-man-than-this" sacrifices on the battlefields.

It may have been nostalgia for such earlier days that moved the Rev. Robert Duncan when he addressed the delegates of the Episcopal Diocese of Delaware at one of their conventions.

"I was raised up to be on center stage in a friendly Christian environment and I find myself on the margin of a hostile and disintegrating society," he said.

Is it possible that the "friendly Christian environment" was just too friendly to too many things and, as a result, became a watered-down version of what it was meant to be?

In the interest of being popular and on amicable terms with "the powers that be," had it become like salt that has lost the qualities which make it salt — and is "thenceforth good for nothing"?

Is it possible that a weakened version of Christianity blessed the very violence, greed, and egocentrism which is rotting society today and making it hostile to the religion that blessed and prayed it into being?

The delegates of the convention referred to the 90s as a "post-Christian era." The term may not be as pessimistic as it may at first seem.

The convention picked up on the brighter side of the words with an implicit acknowledgement that what had been called "Christian" in earlier days may have been a convenient accommodation to the demands of politics, economics, and society.

As the picture took shape in the minds of the delegates, they envisioned the church of the future as "a place where lay people would go on Sunday to get energized for another week of doing what Christ mandated."

This involves actually doing something about the world — not merely blessing institutions of state and business regardless of their damning effect upon the lives of human beings.

If one child in five grows up in poverty, resulting in the stifling of the child's growth and fulfillment, something should be done about the causes.

The convention at times seemed on the edge of a conclusion: If Christianity is to recover its original clout which transformed the world once, it may have to run the risk of becoming unpopular, blessing only what truly deserves blessing, and condemning what should be condemned.

As at all conventions, many good things were said — words which warm the heart and give hope of better days. "We need to consecrate the world to make it holy," declaimed one delegate. "Mission is living your ideals," said Jan Konesey.

Ah, the lovely rhetoric of conventions. But as someone dared ask, "How will it play in the pews?" Max S. Bell, Jr., hazarded the guess that some church people will find this kind of thinking exhilarating. Some others will find it unsettling.

"Consecrate the world to make it holy." It sounds so good— but it's dangerously close to what the church has done in the past — baptizing the unholy as "holy" though it be as profane as hell.

21. The Next World and This

"You people with your Bibles and prayer books and clerical collars ought to quit meddling in what is none of your business." So protested my red-faced, hot-under-the-collar friend.

"What do you mean?" I gulped.

He waved a headline in my face from *USA Today:* "WORSHIPPERS JOIN FIGHT TO SAVE THE EARTH."

"That's what I call meddling," he fairly shouted. "Stick with your own territory — heaven. Leave the earth to people who know what they're doing."

Recovering a bit from the initial onslaught, I said, "But earth's taking a pretty bad drubbing from some of those people who are supposed to know what they're doing."

"All the same, it's not your business. You've got all you can do to prepare people for heaven without getting yourselves all fussed up about earth."

Getting a little more into the swing of this near-frenzied verbal duel, I forced a smile and said, "But we all pray, 'Thy kingdom come; Thy will be done on earth as it is in heaven,' don't we? In fact I've heard the words from your own lips."

"Sure you have, but they're just words for Sunday morning. I'm telling you for your own good — keep your eyes on heaven and don't get tangled up in these earthly things. It's not good for your reputation, and it's bad for your spiritual life."

This all has to do with stories now breaking in a number of papers and magazines, reporting a new, passionate interest among religious folk in what's happening to the earth.

In anticipation of the celebration of Earth Day on April 22, 1991, a spate of books on the environment hit the bookstands and were aired on TV talk shows.

And throughout the country, clergy and laity in synagogues, wayside chapels, and cathedrals mobilized to protect the fragile balances which make this planet habitable.

Recently, an international convocation convened in Moscow. 1,000 participants gathered and issued an eleven-page action plan, calling for a "spiritually-wise, technologically-sound, ethical, and farsighted stewardship of the planet." U. S. astrophysicist Carl Sagan was a participant.

An appeal from the scientists present besought religious leaders to promote among their people an understanding of the planet Earth as "sacred," adding that, "What is regarded as sacred is more likely to be treated with care and respect."

This appeal was referred to the World Council of Churches convocation on "Justice, Peace, and the Integrity of Creation," held recently in Seoul, Korea.

One of the participants at the Global Forum on the Environment and Human Survival in Moscow, the Rev. Glenn E. Olds Jr, a United Methodist who served as ambassador to the United Nations in Geneva, Switzerland, 1969-71, says, "Creation is really a third testament that bears the witness ... of the grace of God."

President of the North American conference on Religion and Ecology, a Catholic priest, the Rev. Donald Conroy, says, "Without an ethical dimension, we won't be able to make the lifestyle changes that are necessary for us to survive."

Canon Jeff Batkin of St. John's Episcopal Cathedral in Jacksonville, Florida, says, "We are stewards of God's creation, and we better start paying attention to it or we're going to be cast out of the garden one more time."

Pope John Paul II devoted a recent message to the environment. The Dalai Lama, 1989 Nobel Prize winner, says, "It is very important that we examine our responsibility and our commitment to values, and think of the kind of world we are to bequeath to future generations."

And leaders of the Moslem faith refer to quotes from the *Koran* such as, "The world is green and beautiful and God has appointed you his stewards over it."

Care of the good earth is an issue which is drawing many diverse faiths together. They may disagree on how to get to heaven, but they seem almost unanimous on how to keep from making a hell of earth.

22.   Is It a Misquote or Just a New Translation?

If somebody misquotes Shakespeare, everybody knows it. If the same person misquotes the Bible, nobody knows it. The reason is that there are so many translations of the Bible that a misquote of the King James Version will be taken as an accurate quote from one of the recent popular versions.

Take for example the lovely 23rd Psalm, which many people know in the 1611 version. Is this a misquote: "Because the Lord is my Shepherd, I have everything I need"?

No — it's a correct quote, but from *The Living Bible,* one of the more modern translations.

Now try this: "He restores my failing health." Misquote? No — just another translation of "He restoreth my soul."

Or let this roll off your tongue, "You provide delicious food for me in the presence of my enemies." Again, not a misquote, but a new translation of "Thou preparest a table before me in the presence of mine enemies."

And now another new translation is coming out, according to an article in the May 20, 1991, issue of *TIME* magazine. The stated objective of the American Bible Society was to make the Holy Scriptures understandable for kids from ages five to thirteen, sometimes known as the Bart Simpson generation.

The translators immersed themselves in the images and lingo of Sesame Street and selected TV cartoons. When the new words and ideas were tested in local churches, adults, jealous of the scriptural advantage being offered children, said they wanted a similar stripped-down model — one even more modern than *The Living Bible.*

So the Bart Simpson generation's Bible, after a few twists and turns of phrase, resulted in the most recent simplification: *The Bible for Today's Family.*

The Old Testament will not be out in this new translation until 1996, but the New Testament version is available now.

So don't think your pastor is misquoting the Bible next Christmas when he reads, "Praise God in heaven! Peace on earth to everyone who pleases God," instead of "Glory to God in the highest, and on earth peace, goodwill toward men." He won't be misquoting, but quoting accurately from the newest translation.

What if we had a dozen or more translations of Shakespeare's "Hamlet" available to help us understand that dramatic moment in the famous soliloquy when Hamlet broods, "To be, or not to be: that is the question . . ."?

Try this on for clarification: "To live or die, that is the issue . . ." Or try this: "Whether I should live out my life with its hardships and embarrassments, or end it: this I must decide." An improvement on Shakespeare's great iambics? A clarification of the issue? Hardly.

If this newest translation of the scriptures began with the idea of making the Bible more understandable to children and teenagers by employing modern vernacular and streamlining the vocabulary, what about the polysyllabic verbs and nouns dripping from the lips of modern kids as they discuss video, computers, softwear, and such. Don't worry about the kids — they'll be there ahead of some of us.

The multiple new translations of the Bible frequently eliminate or alter words which have distinct historical and theological meaning and are as irreplaceable as the word electricity.

For example, this new Bible drops the word *righteousness* — one of the great words of the Judeo-Christian tradition, a word which means correspondence with the divine will.

The word *grace*, representing the core of much of the New Testament, is replaced by the bland word *kindness* — a good enough word, but totally inadequate to cover the concept of God's unmerited love for mankind.

In many of the new translations also, "Thou" as an address to God is substituted by the familiar — if not too familiar — word *you.* The chummy pronoun is used in some pastoral prayers — leaving many worshippers feeling they are crouched beneath low ceilings where once great arches of faith reached heaven-ward.

Let us not forsake the "more stately mansions" of our English language just to make more plain what is — and has long been — plain enough.

23.   No Church Has a Monopoly on the Holy Spirit

Here are some points from "The Devil's Bible" (which I haven't finished writing yet): HOW TO DESTROY A FAITH IN ITS EARLY PHASES:

1. Let a small group of devout individuals have a genuine religious experience, one that is vital and throbbing with life.

2. Let them formalize it.

3. Let them intellectualize it and drain off its emotional content.

4. Let them organize it.

5. Let them spiritualize it and purge it of all "taint" of the physical.

6. Let them train experts to interpret it for the benefit of "ordinary people."

7. Let them sanctify it and set it aside from everyday life.

8. Let them pray and worship in their holy place as though there were no other people on the face of the earth as devoted as they are.

9. Let them set their stamp of identity upon it so that it will not be confused with any other kind of religious experience.

10. Let them keep it to themselves as a sacred trust.

11. Let them assume an air of sophistication so as to win the approval of an enlightened world.

12. Let them not hold opinions that would conflict with the trends of the times.

It's a known and bemoaned fact that many of the "mainline denominations" are not holding their own in the modern world, while many independent movements are flourishing — perhaps largely because the traditional churches are afraid to accept some of the values and insights of non-traditional groups, which seem to be making a difference in the way people live and move and have their being.

Recently in Brighton, England, the Archbishop of Canterbury, George Carey, lauded the charismatic movement. Speaking before an assembly of 2,500 Catholics, Anglicans, Presbyterians, and independent Pentecostals, he praised the movement for its "great blessings to us all." Acknowledging that the movement has its flaws, he urged the convocation not to let the flaws blind them to its genuine contributions.

In an interview on BBC following his address, Carey defended his own outspoken identification with charismatics. "It's the fastest-growing section of the religious community," he said. "We must listen to what it's saying to us."

At the Brighton convocation, Pope John Paul II's personal chaplain, Raneiro Cantalammessa, confessed from the pulpit: "[I] have sinned against the unity of the Body of Christ (by not accepting Protestants as part of the church). No church has a monopoly on the Holy Spirit."

With such things occurring on a world scale, there's hope that the Christian religion might recover from its centuries-long schizoid illness.

The successful churches in this part of the 20th Century are whole churches ministering to the whole man. *TIME* magazine of August 5, 1991 reports a trend which may well take hold nationally. In a spiritual ambiance which reconciles intellect and emotion, spiritual and physical, religion and everyday life, at the Second Baptist Church of Houston, Texas, there are weight rooms for exercise, saunas for physical relaxation from stressful days, and outdoor and indoor gardens where people can sit, converse, relax, and meditate.

In North Phoenix, Arizona, there's a church which has its own gym, roller rink, and racquetball courts to minister to the body while ministering to the soul — and serving the reconciling function of bringing both together in the name of God.

These things can happen best in large churches, naturally, but they can happen in smaller churches as well, at least in part, and to the degree that religion drops its barriers and reaches out to all of life.

Taking the best that all denominations have to offer, rising above exclusive, parochial attitudes, churches of the future may well be positioned to minister to the needs of whole human beings who then can love God with all their heart, soul, mind, and strength . . . and their neighbor as themselves.

24.   Where Satan Dwells

Serious efforts have been mounted lately to hunt the devil down to his dark lair and zap his diabolical majesty. Or, falling short of this, to be able to say: "Here he is! We've got him cornered!"

A full-length article in a news magazine recently dealt with the phenomenon of evil, using Saddam Hussein and Adolph Hitler as examples.

Fascination with the subject is more than merely academic.

Throughout the world, thousands of people are prepared to confess they have at times met up with something which has the feel of malicious evil intent upon their undoing.

The theme is perennial, from Goethe's *Faust* to C. S. Lewis' *Screwtape Letters* in which two evil spirits, Screwtape and Wormwood, conspire to engineer the fall of an unsuspecting good man.

On the lighter side, there is Douglas Wallop's *The Year the Yankees Lost the Pennant*. This book gave us the successful Broadway play, "Damn Yankees," in which the author has a slinking character crawl up out of a city sewer to make a deal with a frustrated middle-aged male, making him a baseball hero in exchange for his soul.

Perhaps the most bizarre and lurid treatment of the subject of evil was aired in a recent "20/20" TV show hosted by Hugh Downes and Barbara Walters.

Before the eyes of millions of viewers an emotionally-disturbed teenage girl, who went by the name of Gina, was subjected to the medieval rite of exorcism.

Prior to the exorcism ceremony Gina had been under the care of a psychiatrist for her disturbed behavior, which included wild emotional outbursts and obscenities. Following the exorcism ritual the girl was returned to Miami Children's Hospital for continued treatment.

The whole thing seems to have started with Cardinal John O'Connor, the archbishop of New York, who has been attempting to restore the ancient rite to modern acceptance.

In a sermon, O'Connor warned his congregation that the devil is still at work in the world, and that he, O'Connor, had personally authorized two exorcisms to take place in his diocese. It was with the consent of a consultant to the archbishop that the TV exorcism was made public.

Far from being fully and enthusiastically endorsed by the Catholic Church, some Catholic theologians were outraged by the TV show.

"Televising this was indefensible," declared the Rev. Richard McBrien, chairman of the theology department of the University of Notre Dame. "To sprinkle holy water over serious and complex problems is to trivialize them and ensure that they continue."

But O'Connor and others are not alone in their preoccupation with the devil and his minions. According to the April 15, 1991 issue of *Newsweek*, a Gallup poll taken in 1990 revealed that 55 percent of the respondents believed in Satan, and 49 percent said they thought people are sometimes possessed by the devil.

This may say something about the influence of religion upon sensitive persons — old and young alike. In all denominations there are judgmental, guilt-producing nuances, which tend to create fear and a sense of unworthiness — even self-rejection in some individuals — turning them against themselves, and turning others of less-tender consciences, into sadistic inquisitors bearing the bad news of judgment and damnation to sensitive souls.

The young girl called Gina, like many other impressionable young people, may well be a victim of this kind of judgmental and punitive religious education.

On the other hand, in all denominations there is the kind of religious nuance which lends support to human beings with all their uncertainties and misgivings, helping them to accept themselves as accepted by the God who created and loves them — body and soul, and offers them grace for the living of their lives.

The devil which some persons undertake to exorcise may be no devil at all, but the pathetic disturbed behavior of tender souls who have been confused and misled by barrels of religious mumbo-jumbo.

There is evil in the world, and plenty of it. But to look for it in some poor disturbed 16-year-old girl, who goes by the name of Gina, may serve only to divert attention from the devil's real address. This is in the minds of human beings who use other human beings for their own egocentric purposes — from Adolph Hitler and Saddam Hussein to ecclesiastics of any denomination who aspire to make a name for themselves at the expense of the weak, the poor, and the downtrodden.

25.   Planning to Go to Heaven?

Do you believe in heaven? Are you planning to go there when the trumpet sounds and heavenly music flows down over the celestial battlements?

And hell? If you believe in the place of everlasting torment, but don't think the eternal fires are being stoked for you, who on earth would you have go there?

According to a recent Gallup survey, more Americans believe in both heaven and hell than did so in 1952. The latest poll shows that 78% of these questioned declared they not only believe in heaven, but feel sure they're headed in that direction.

The survey reveals that 60% of those who responded actually believe in hell (that's slightly above the 1952 figure) —but only 4% think they're destined for the hotter climes.

These questions and answers trigger other questions. So with those Gallup poll respondents still in mind, here are a few "follow-ups":

1. If you believe in heaven and that you're going there, who's nominating you? Suppose self-nominations don't count. Could you round up at least a half-dozen persons to put your name up?

2. If you could manage to get your six together, would you be willing to level with them — let them in on what kind of person you really are, beneath all your "nice" appearances?

3. Would you be happy to leave the final decision up to One "before whom all hearts are open, all desires known, and from whom no secrets are hid"?

4. Have you done anything this past week to make your bit of earth a bit of heaven-on-earth? Or have you made your part of earth a piece of hell, and so want to get out of it?

5. Are you just plain world weary, tired of the fight, don't want to continue the struggle with evil in your own nature and in the world? If this is the case, you may fancy you are being lifted on the wings of angels, but they're only chicken wings. In other words, you're chickening out, my friend.

6. Could it be that your notion that you are worthy of heaven is your way of distancing yourself from some people you don't like — your logic being, "I'm good enough for heaven, but they're not!" This would be just one more cheap way of feeling superior,

and shows of superiority may not be welcome in the humble kingdom of God.

7. If you believe in hell but don't think you're going there, in heaven's name, who do you think is? Who are those 56% destined to weeping, wailing, and gnashing of teeth? Is it possible that you are on some self-appointed nominating committee prepared, at the blink of an eye, to put up the names of a few of your favorite enemies?

8. If you should get to heaven and at one of the celestial banquets you are seated next to somebody you never liked, would you ask some lovely ministering angel to change your place at the table?

9. If you want to go to heaven in the hope you'd be reunited with some of your "dear dead loved ones," have you made your peace with them, found forgiveness in your heart for their earthly offenses against you? You'd no doubt be miserable, even in heaven, if you haven't done this earthly homework.

10. Now about those people who you feel certain are going to hell — what are you doing to help them find the fire escape? It may well be that one of the qualifications for your entrance into the blessed kingdom is some sort of volunteer service on a rescue squad.

So, thanks to Mr. Gallup and his pollsters and the hundreds of respondents who in the clatter and clang of a busy world have reminded us all of the eternal dimensions of human existence and have raised questions beyond questions and hinted at answers beyond answers.

26.　　　God — Male or Female?

WHO IS GOD? The question in large white capitals against a night sky filled with stars appeared on the cover of December 1990 *LIFE* magazine, introducing the lead article.

The title piqued my curiosity, but something about it offended me. What bothered me was the almost-too-familiar way it was put — as though God were just another personality at a crowded New Year's Eve party with the curious staring and asking each other, "Who's that?"

Another bit of news struck me the same way. A release in *National And International Religion Report* of November 19, 1990 states that at its 1992 General Conference, the United Methodist Church will decide whether God is male or female, or something else.

This is like standing on a street corner, watching all the girls and guys go by, some looking like male, some female, and now and then one who looks like neither one — or both. You glance at a friend and ask, "Is that . . . ?"

All of the frenzy and furor come as a result of certain feminine protests that God is nearly always referred to in the Bible and church liturgy as male.

I'm confident the subject will be handled in the most erudite manner, with all the latest findings of theology, psychology, and other disciplines cited by various speakers.

But after all's said and done, the entire debate must tumble into the annals of trivia, nonsense, and perhaps irreverence.

In this last half of the 20th Century we humans have become so caught up in the biological differences between male and female that we just can't seem to get over it. It's as though gender had just been discovered and it's the hottest news in town. Even God seems not to be exempt from the gender flap. Which side is God on — male or female? Strident voices want the divine to level with us on the subject.

The closer the question is pushed to the biological, the sillier it seems. Sex is a function of flesh and blood existence, designed mainly, so it would seem, for the purpose of reproduction and the ongoing of the human and other species, with a pleasure bonus built in as further inducement to perpetuate life on this planet.

"But the Bible refers to God as he, doesn't it?" It certainly does. "And doesn't it speak of God as Father?" Truly and beautifully, it does. "So . . . ?"

The Bible also says, "The Lord is my shepherd . . ." But would anyone presume to log this in God's record — "God, occupation: shepherd?"

Should we pursue the question of God's gender to the point

of absurdity, or should we accept a useful and reverent simile or metaphor — that God is *like* a caring, compassionate father, and let it go at that?

If we insist upon keeping the Ultimate Reality tied down to our human concepts with their preferences and prejudices, warps, limitations, and distortions, we will find ourselves — or be found — worshipping not God but our own ideas of God which suit our gender, class, nationality, or whatever.

Individuals and nations want God to pass through some "Ellis Island" naturalization experience. We don't want any alien tendencies in God. God must be my God, with my gender as preference. God must be all American for us Americans, with all "unAmerican" biases or propensities confessed and duly recanted.

One of the most misunderstood books of the Old Testament, the Book of Jonah, presents a man to whom the very idea that Jehovah, the God of Israel, might be interested in saving Nineveh, the capital of the enemy nation, was an outrage — a totally unthinkable, unworthy, unacceptable thought.

The fury of war — is intensified in its horror to the extent that religion becomes part of the battle cry. As each opposing nation hates the other with a holy hatred, in the name of a god they have naturalized, each has tried to make him its own so as to accommodate its own aims and purposes.

27.   Pull Out All the Stops, It's Christmas!

Like everything else in a cockeyed, controversial world, Christmas is speared on the spit of public debate and poked into the fires of controversy.

It's just not right and proper — even honest-to-goodness "American" to celebrate the birth of Christ with manger scenes in public places, on land "owned" by taxpayers of all religious persuasions.

Some small measure of "peace on earth, good will toward

men" has been achieved in some cities, towns, and hamlets by the authorities declaring it's okay to have a creche or nativity scene on public land — provided there is a "secular" symbol like a Christmas tree standing beside it.

OK, add Santa Claus and Rudolph the red-nosed reindeer." Have Bing Crosby on tape singing "White Christmas." Whatever it takes to "prove" the display is not just plain "religious" will get it off the hook.

So, what's new? This is the happy mixture of sights and sounds and symbols most of us have called Christmas since we were kids. We've never known it otherwise.

Christmas purists who are offended by the "secular" ambience of the celebration may not know what they're asking for.

For several years I served as a member of Wilmington, Delaware's "Keep Christ In Christmas" committee. The yuletide project involved the erection and "peopling" of a creche in one of the city's public parks.

The movement grew out of a fear that the "real" meaning of Christmas might be lost in the secular hurly-burly. Paradoxically, this same fear in the past, carried to a paranoid extreme, struck a near-death blow to the happy season that glows like a friendly fire in the midst of winter's gray world.

During the reign of Oliver Cromwell in 17th Century England, Christmas was banned by parliament. And in our own New England, in the early days, the celebration was forbidden.

The rollicking joy of the season was too strong for the pious palates of our puritan ancestors, it seems. To have the birth of mankind's savior celebrated with customs borrowed from the pagan world put too much of a strain on their brand of piety.

Of course, there's little room for doubt about December 25 being the date of ancient man's celebration of the winter solstice, when the sun seemed frighteningly remote, and ancient tribes held their festivals in the hope that the bright light would not completely forsake them, but come again with another springtime.

Ancient Persians celebrated the 25th of December as the birthday of the unconquerable sun. And when the Christian Church sought a desirable day to mark the birthday of Jesus, it deliberately and without apology embraced the pagan exuberance and hope gathered about that date, and baptized it into the Christian faith.

The season's merriment and the custom of giving gifts, especially to children, reflects the Roman Saturnalia, celebrated in ancient Rome from December 17 to 24.

When we "deck the halls with boughs of holly" and light our Christmas candles, we're unashamedly throwing Christian arms about a pagan celebration of pre-Christian Rome.

Some of our colorful yuletide customs have Germanic and Celtic origins which originally had nothing to do with the birth of Jesus in the little town of Bethlehem. They merely represented the most joyous and hopeful moods of the pagan world.

So bring in the Christmas tree, the yule log, the holly, and the laurel. Bring in whatever light cheered the world before the real light came.

Pull out all the stops of the mighty organ of human hopes and joys, and let us sing, "Joy to the world, the Lord is come!"

28.   Christmas Carols Over Lenin's Tomb

Christmas carols in Red Square! Can you believe it? The sweet, reassuring sounds of a believing world echoing over that austere quadrangle of Russia where the flagrant faithlessness of a nation has been flaunted and paraded for more than seventy years.

Red Square: Lenin's tomb, military pomp, tanks and missile carriers rumbling past. In a high reviewing stand the mighty of the mighty signal their approval as uniformed men march by. This is Red Square. But Christmas carols?

Now if you're talking about Christmas carols in Times Square in the Big Apple, or Manger Square in Bethlehem, or St. Marks Square in Venice, with all the church bells of the ancient city by the sea sounding over the Adriatic — that's one thing. But Red

Square in Moscow?

Is it possible that George Cornell of the Associated Press made a mistake? Or could it be a Yuletide spoof — something to smile about in a not-too-cheerful Christmas season?

But no. In all seriousness and with his usual reporting accuracy, Cornell says it happened. From December 20 to January 7, 1991, Christmas was celebrated in Red Square.

Imagine: lights on trees, cathedral bells ringing, community caroling. And imagine this: The Soviet navy band playing "Silent Night" and "Hark, The Herald Angles Sing."

Last year nothing like this happened. And the year before last. For over seventy years it hadn't happened. Why now?

Well, it seems Russia is different now. Secular icons reared to replace sacred icons have fallen. The great names, along with their heroic statues, have toppled. The Russian economy has crumbled. Citizens of Moscow and Leningrad wait in lines for food that never comes.

Lenin, Stalin, and Brezhnev — names to conjure with in the past — are now forgotten, and happily so. But in the Russian soul there is a name which has survived the godless years. Muscovites sang that name in Red Square last Christmas season — the name of a child born in a little town called Bethlehem nearly 2,000 years ago.

In those 2,000 years kings and kingdoms have come and gone. Conquerors have conquered and been conquered. Those who have lived by the sword have died by the sword.

The unforgettable name, the name which sets the human heart to singing, belongs to one who came to establish another kind of kingdom. He called it The Kingdom of God.

It is a kingdom of love, mercy, compassion; and only those whom life has meekened can enter. The power-seekers, the arrogant, the proud, the mighty are outside its gates.

It seems that when reality humbles us — as reality has a way of doing, and when it reveals our deepest human needs, we are ready for the better kingdom.

Just such a time of revelation has come to Russia, and it may be that it is nearer The Kingdom of God than many of its people dared think it would be as they witnessed their churches burning, their clergy deported and executed.

According to Cornell, the Christmas celebration in Red Square featured gifts for orphans, the sick, and handicapped. The ceremonies concluded on January 7 with a service of prayer and thanksgiving.

The celebration was sponsored by The Soviet-U.S. Joint Conference on Charitable Cooperation, headed by U. S. Episcopal priest J.S. Cantry.

Who knows but the Christmas celebration in Red Square may rekindle fires of faith in places far and near — places where the carols of Christmas have never been silenced, and so have become little more than commercial ploys to put people like us in the mood of buying more and more of what people need less and less — and often in the spirit of "Let's get it over with!"

29.   A Human Story

Tell the story. Write it in antique calligraphy. Embellish the caps. Emblazon the page margins with gold leaf. Let it be removed from the hard world of human conflict, greed, power, suspicion, and distrust — all that would sully its purity.

Let the radiance of a star fall upon the quiet pastoral scene where awed shepherds and august wise men from the East gather to do obeisance to an infant cradled in his mother's arms, while the pensive figure of a young carpenter from Nazareth stands protectively by.

And angels — let there be angels from the realms of glory, singing in celestial chorus above the scene, harmonizing with the mother's lullaby to her baby.

Bring in a sheep or two, and perhaps a donkey to complete the tableau. Then let the bells in church towers ring, and gifts be exchanged; and let there be smiles and happy voices. Christmas — the festival of a joyful faith, the celebration of the soul's fondest hopes.

But hark! Stirring through the holy radiance there is a dark rumor which may, for some, tarnish the halo above the young woman's head.

It seems there was an unexpected, unexplained pregnancy. Young Mary of Nazareth, to whom he was engaged, was with child, and he, Joseph, the village carpenter, was not the father. He protested that he was not, and Mary agreed that he was not.

The man was offended, angered, and considered the two honorable courses open to him in the strict moral and religious code of the day. Either expose his bride-to-be, and have the righteous will of the community fall upon her, or call off the engagement, the equivalent of a divorce, leaving mother and child under a cloud the rest of their lives.

It was a time of tension and suspicion between the man and woman, days of mental agony and nights of disturbed sleep. In a troubled dream, the young carpenter was assured that the child of Mary was the son of God. Accepting the dream's assurance, Joseph assumed responsibility for the child's life and the life of the mother.

Forget angels for a moment, and you have a very sensitive human situation which may represent one of the sacred story's most poignantly significant themes: a woman confessing pregnancy and at the same time declaring innocence of infidelity to the man she was to marry; a male ego — hurt, outraged, and angered — coming under control and accepting a child admittedly not his own.

Consider for a moment the possibilities of recurring tension between man and growing boy in the years to come. Add to the tension the feeling of rejection that must have surfaced in the mind of the boy as he observed the marked difference between Joseph's treatment of the other children in the household and him. These dynamics are well documented in such family relationships, and it is a well-known fact that they leave their wounds in the psyche of the rejected one.

The inevitable question, "Who is my father?" no doubt was wrung from the soul of the boy on one of those days in Nazareth when he was growing up. In the name of that lonely boy, and the man he became, every human being who has ever wondered about unequal treatment among children of the same family, and asked that same question, has a right to the same answer.

In the name of that young woman, Mary, any teenage girl, pregnant before marriage, experiencing the shame and rejection of family and society, can take hope. Such wounding experience can — through her dedication to the life of her child, as one who belongs to God — turn shame into glory, and a blessing to mankind.

Read it over and over again and, for a thoughtful moment, let the human side of this divine story humanize you anew, and help you to see the divine possibilities of human life in the hands of God. (Matthew 1: 18-21)

30. Alien Altars for Christian Worship

Imagine a group of United Methodists, followers of the proper Englishman, John Wesley, sitting crosslegged in a circle in a remote woods with a bonfire burning a hole in the dusk.

The group is chanting rhythmically, some perhaps dancing, Indian fashion, around the circle's flaming hub, their faces painted with bright colorful clays, moccasined feet beating time with the ancient rhythm of drums.

It is the sacrament of the green corn, a native American ceremony. Positioned significantly within the circle are "sacramentals" — mud, bread, mashed strawberries, ashes, and a feather from the wing of an eagle. Excluded only for health reasons, pipes, part of the sacramental elements, will not be smoked.

This ceremony may become part of United Methodist worship if a report, accepted by a 23-member panel, is accepted by the denomination's General Conference meeting in Louisville, Kentucky, in the summer of 1992, and made part of the *Book of Worship.*

For one of the few times in the church's life, the pure stream of Christian ritual will mingle with pagan ceremony. Some who favor the move contend that this will enable the 29,000 native Americans in the United Methodist Church to share their heritage with the rest of the church.

On the other hand, there are those who fear a possible erosion of Christian beliefs through such a cordial relationship of pagan and Christian elements. These people promise to make their protests heard at the Louisville General Conference.

Alien as it may seem in the context of traditional Christian worship, there is something to be said for the proposal.

In imagining the scene of the green corn ceremony, let the participants be youth at a camp beside the Chester River or on the Chesapeake Bay. Let the dancers be lithe young bodies swaying and weaving through the firelight. Let the pagan symbols of mud, bread, and ashes mingle with the Christian symbols of bread and wine. Let the mashed strawberries represent the sacrifice of Christ on behalf of mankind. The youthful voices chanting through the dusk, the fire flickering upon painted faces. A lasting impression will be created that will linger through the years. The experience will be carried back to local churches and reenacted again and again.

Let the ceremony remind the youth of their relationship with earth — and fire and water and sky. Let them feel the sacredness of the ground beneath their dancing feet, all the natural elements which sustain life on the planet Earth — corn waving in the fields, the beaver in a log-choked stream, fish leaping in the river. If this can happen, a generation of youth may be saved to help save the earth.

"But," say a chorus of sober voices, "imagine another picture: a group of youth caught up in the primal rhythm and imagery, the passion of youth mingling with the passion of chants and drum beats, and all of the strange gods of earth and field and forest come rushing in and join the celebration, then the Christian symbolism is swamped in a torrent of pagan orgy."

Those who advance such a caveat — and they are ready and armed for battle — will have strong allies in the prophets of ancient Israel who stormed and vented their righteous wrath against their own people who fell into the practice of mingling their devotion to Jehovah with the religion of Baal, with its groves and mountain-top shrines and orgiastic fertility rituals.

Opponents of the inclusion of the green corn ceremony in the *Book of Worship of United Methodism* may well take the position of Israel's great prophets in their battle against what they may regard as a dangerous syncretism, the mingling of two different, and apparently contradictory, streams of religious thought and practice.

Whatever the outcome of the General Conference, there's bound to be difficulty in getting these two sides of a controversial issue to sit down and smoke the peace pipe together.

31.   Alternatives to God?

Can Alcoholics Anonymous get along without their "higher power"? They say they can't — that this reference and deference to God is an essential part of their 12-point program, which has successfully helped alcohol-addicted individuals get control of their lives.

But some alcoholics have left the organization, because the religious aspect of the group's discipline offended them. They claim they can get along quite well without God — that they can control themselves without any "outside help," thank you.

For over 50 years, AA has been recognized as the most effective way to get control of compulsive drinking. Although the success rate is not perfect, it is better than any other approach to the problem. Twenty-nine percent of its membership have been in control of their drinking habit for a five-year period.

Now, two new approaches are being offered to people for whom God or the "higher power" is an obstacle.

One of these new programs is called RR or Rational Recovery. The lingo which gives voice to Rational Recovery may seem less than rational to some ears. Take for example this bit of advice from a group monitor, Jim Petermann, to a female participant: "Haul your beast out of the cellar. Beat up on her, confront her. Then lock her back up. Beating up on your beast is a serious tool." Rational?

To people acquainted with the Judeo-Christian tradition, this sounds like beating up on the devil — making evil the focus of attention instead of good. Substituting a lower power for the "higher power."

Historically, it has been people who had trouble in accepting "the God part" who have dropped out of AA. "They were praying and talking about God half the time at the meetings I went to," complained John Norfolk, a Maryland resident who won a 1988 suit against being ordered by a judge to attend AA after being convicted of drunk driving. He complained that his civil rights had been abridged by having to be part of a group which appeals to God for help.

James Christopher, founder of SOS, Secular Organization for Sobriety, which claims an international membership of 20,000, says, "We credit ourselves for achieving sobriety."

"The whole higher-power concept just never did it for me," says Paul, a 45-year-old mechanic from Brockton, Massachusetts, who bounced in and out of AA for twelve years before leaving it finally and joining a Boston-based organization.

From an outside view, it seems that the reason some people leave AA — because they don't want to feel dependent upon a higher power than themselves — is the same reason people leave religion and the church. They want to be in control of their lives without any help from anyone.

The "I can-handle-it" attitude of some of these new groups seems perilously like the attitude which led to the trouble in the first place.

As Dr. Edward Khantzian, a psychiatrist at the Danvers State and Cambridge Hospitals in Massachussets, says about addicted people: "They need an antidote for the terrible, progressive self-centeredness that develops with this addictive illness."

This kind of self-centeredness afflicts many people, alcoholics and otherwise "normal" people alike. There is something about us human beings that wants to be all-in-all to ourselves. In a word, something that wants to be God, and it bothers us when we think we're not.

Much of the healing power of AA and religion is the escape from the ego trap with all its fears, frustrations, and prejudices, through faith in something greater than ego.

For any group or individual to turn away from that redeeming escape is to land up in the psychic hell from which some other escape is bound to be attempted.

32. Down to Earth Worship

A Christian church, where the worship of God is forbidden, exists and is flourishing in the city of Sverdlovsk in the Ural Mountains of central Russia.

The church was founded on October 24, 1990 when it was legally recognized. Since then it has grown to a membership of 600 devoted followers of the faith.

"We are allowed one prayer at the beginning and one prayer at the end, and we have discussions but not worship," says 34-year old Lydia Istomina, the congregation's lay leader, a former college administrator.

The church without a church — that is without a building called "the church" — meets in public buildings, whose state ownership places the no-worship restriction upon the new congregation.

While plans are under way for the congregation to have a sanctuary and an affiliated school, it could be hoped that this dynamic group might not become formalized too soon. The freedom to worship in the conventional sense could dry up the springs of spontaneity and creativity, which are the life of the young group.

Bishop Hans Vaxby of the Northern Europe Area of the United Methodist Church says that Sverdlovsk is an important pilot project for other areas in the Soviet Union, because it is open, community-oriented and sensitive to the needs of the younger Soviet generation that has no experience with religion.

"We may have discussions but not worship." This very restriction may be the church's greatest advantage. The door to formal worship is closed, but the door to discussion is open. This means they have the freedom to talk together warmly, frankly, and openly about God and their faith and all the other questions which the human mind grapples with when it is free to express itself.

These are the matters which in formal worship are left to the professional cleric, standing in the high pulpit and before the high altar, to deal with, interpret, and expound upon.

Now, put all this in the hands of people who want to explore faith and the meaning of life, and all kinds of marvelous experiences are possible. Not one mind addressing the multitudes but certain persons in the multitudes speaking to the multitudes, people talking to people, revealing their innermost being to one another.

By definition, *discussion* is earnest conversation. This group meeting in the Ural Mountains, limited in their religious gatherings to discussion, have found the wings of the human spirit.

Long before the inception of the formal differentiation between clergy and laity, all were laity. The people of faith, shared their experiences of faith with one another. They were lifted on the wings of their shared faith into a higher life. When all of that thought and feeling is narrowed down to the thoughts and feelings of one individual, however well-trained and dedicated, something marvelous and powerful is lost.

Worship, as traditionally practiced, is under the direction of one individual — priest, minister, or rabbi. The sacred words are his or hers to speak; the powerful symbolism of communication with God is enacted by the clergy, usually attired in vestments, which set the professional apart as the sole representative of the divine.

Who assumes this role, the focus of formal worship, when worship itself is forbidden? The people! People who believe that God is near to each of them as they are near to one another and that they have the right to stand before God as a group and speak for themselves, with themselves, and on behalf of themselves.

Discussion — the rare act of faith permitted to those Ural Mountain people — may be the one element lacking in the traditional, formal church.

It is the secret of success for many modern support groups, including Alcoholics Anonymous. Frank, open, earnest conversations, which lower the barriers between people, may well be the secret of the renewal of the church in the modern world, as it was the life force which gave birth to the church originally.

This kind of face-to-face, honest-to-God conversation may well be one of the overlooked sacraments, a dimension of communion forgotten in the church's zeal to organize, formalize, and succeed.

33.   Where Differences Dissolve

Something excitingly spiritual is happening in what some think is one of the most God-forsaken areas in the whole country.

Out in our Pacific Northwest, where only a meager 3% of the state of Washington's residents show their faces in any church. Out there.

And Oregon, its neighbor state, has next to the lowest church attendance in the nation. Out there.

It seems that it all started when Joe Aldrich, President of Multnomah School of the Bible in Portland, Oregon found it hard to sleep nights with those depressing figures on his mind.

So, about eighteen months ago he called a meeting of all ministers in the Salem, Oregon area. They met over a four-day period in a desolate spot on the Oregon coast.

It was not your regular "preachers meeting" where "the brethren" edify their egos by celebrating personal achievements and indulging in "what I told my people last Sunday." None of the typical "preacher stuff."

Instead they prayed, sang their hymns, shared their discouragements and fears, their sins and guilt with one another —and found forgiveness and reconciliation.

What a denominational potpourri it was: Presbyterians, Methodists, Lutherans, charismatics, Pentecostals. All of the historic splits and rents in the whole cloth of original Christianity. All the makings of bedlam, but no bedlam.

As they met together day after day, night after night, the differences dissolved, vanished, as though they had never been.

To date nearly 500 ministers from Oregon and Washington have participated in similar gatherings in eighteen cities and rural areas.

In these sessions the participants confess their weaknesses, temptations, and sins to one another. Opening up. Letting down. Throwing off the painful silence of concealed guilt and fear.

At one point in a meeting an Assembly of God clergyman stood with tears in his eyes and confessed that he was guilty of judging a conservative Baptist colleague who was present.

With this, the Baptist was on his feet asking the other man's forgiveness for having done the same to him. The two men met in the center of the room and embraced.

In one of these gatherings a chair was placed in the center of a circle and individual participants would voluntarily take the chair and openly confess their deepest needs.

Some were struggling with their marriages. Some who had been reared in homes of alcoholic parents were desperately reaching out for love. Some were struggling with their own carnal natures.

As one man after another shared his needs, others would surround him in prayerful support and acceptance.

It's happening in the Northwest. It could happen here — and it well may. Wherever two or three — or more — meet together in honest-to-God confrontation of their own faults and sins, and in humility lay bare their weaknesses to one another, it can happen.

Is it possible that the time has come when the differences which alienate and divide people from people — paradoxically "in the name of God" — might melt away, and become differences which weld together, enhance, and reconcile?

If it can happen with clergy, it can happen with congregations and parishes. So bring the Lutherans, Baptists, Methodists, Assembly of God, and all the rest together, and let each share what each has found in separate pursuits of God and His will.

Bring it all together. This will help a world and let it all be shared in humility and thanksgiving to God.

34. Religion Makes a Big Difference — For Some People

After all's said and done, does religion make any difference in what people do or don't do?

As the altar candles die in tiny wisps of smoke. After the last notes of the pipe organ tremble away into silence. When the sacred book is closed, the vestments are hung reverently in their place, and the people who gathered have dispersed, what difference does it make?

If you believe the figures in a recent survey by the Barna Research Group, a sixty-page report titled "The Church Today," you'll say that most Americans think churches are irrelevant and ineffective. You'll say that even the clergy feel the church has "little positive impact on souls and society." (56%, according to the report.)

Now this doesn't mean that Americans are not what you'd call religious. Like the ancient Athenians, they're "very religious" in their way.

In 1989, religious radio was the third most common program format in the industry. More than 1,100 stations were broadcasting the Christian gospel in some form, and people were listening.

Add to this the audience tuned into 350 TV stations which beam religious shows across the country.

In the money department, religious folk give more than thirty billion dollars to Christian churches each year.

And nobody can say we lack places of worship in America. We have 350,000 of them — Protestant and Catholic alike. That gives us forty times as many churches as Mc Donald's fast-food outlets.

Are the twin arches making more of an impression than the gilded crosses? People buy, consume, and assimilate — and somehow manage to live by the strength of Big Macs and Quarter Pounders from Mc Donald's.

What about the bread of life they get from the churches? Do they squeeze it into a little round ball and drop it into the nearest trash can?

The report says that although Americans "see the Bible as accurate, relevant, and helpful, they have problems making time to study it, concentrating enough to comprehend it, committing themselves sufficiently to adhere to it, or jeopardizing their social status by openly supporting it."

Which may suggest that you shouldn't expect to see throngs of strong, courageous, caring people marching through the church doors, eager to do battle with evil and injustice.

But wait, there's a better story to tell, according to *The*

United Methodist Reporter. It reaches back to World War II, when France's Vichy government was deporting 80,000 Jews to Nazi death camps.

In the village of Le-Chambon lived a small group of deeply religious folk who risked their lives to rescue many of these people and keep them out of harm's way.

Pierre Sauvage, motion picture producer-director, was an infant among the Jewish refugees sheltered by these good people.

When Sauvage returned to the village that saved him, he had a haunting question on his mind — Why had they done it?

The answer was important to him personally and as producer-director of the movie he was making, "Weapons of the Spirit," which traces his own odyssey against the backdrop of goodness in the midst of evil.

He says, "The single most striking thing about these people is the way they view what they did as being absolutely natural."

They are descendants of the Huguenots, French Protestants, who themselves suffered persecution for centuries. When Sauvage asks them why they took such enormous risks to shelter him and other Jews, they shrug and tell him, "We helped because they needed to be helped. It was just the right thing to do."

Another person who owes his life to these folk calls them "the most solid people on earth."

For some people, religion makes a difference. They may be a minority, but they are a dynamic minority. They may work silently, like yeast in dough, but wherever they are, the world feels their presence without ever really understanding the power working within them.

35.   Pray Your Prayers and Take Your Pills

"Take two aspirins, say your prayers, and call me in the morning."

Believe it or not, you may hear something like this when you call your doctor in the future.

The area between mind and body has long been a kind of No Man's Land for the medical profession, an area claimed by religious quacks, and vulgarized by spectacular "healings."

But the connections between thought, feeling, and health have been begging for an honest investigation, and at last they're getting just that.

Mind/body medicine was the topic of a weekend conference in Boston recently, under the sponsorship of the University of Massachusetts Medical School and the American Holistic Medical Association.

Dr. Herbert Benson of the Harvard Medical School, director of the Mind/Body Medical Institute at New England Deaconess Hospital in Boston, has been one of the pioneers in mind/body research.

With him was Dr. Deepak Chopra, who told the conference, "In the East, we say if you want to know what your mind was like in the past, examine your body now. If you want to know what your body will look like in the future, examine your mind now."

What has been the delay in mainstream medicine's acknowledgement of the intimate relationship between what we think and the condition of our physical health?

The answer is a reasonable one. Scientists, being scientists, needed sufficient proof that there is more to disease than meets the lenses of their microscopes.

Now, it is reported, doctors know from precise, controlled, observable studies that the body makes specific chemicals in response to thoughts and emotions. These chemicals, so runs the explanation, communicate what you and I are thinking and feeling to the cells of our bodies by way of networks between brain, heart, blood vessels, stomach, intestines, and the immune system.

Commenting on this subtle network, Dr. Chopra said, "That means the immune system is essentially eavesdropping on the internal dialogue of the mind. And when you say you have a *gut feeling,* you're not speaking metaphorically anymore."

The good news in all this was reported by Dr. Benson, who told the conference that whatever damage the mind does to our bodies through deleterious thought processes, it can undo through what he calls relaxation response.

This is very simple, he says. Just sit quietly, close your eyes and breathe slowly. With each breath out, repeat silently a word or phrase, perhaps a brief prayer. Do this twice a day for about twenty minutes at a time.

Benson says, "About 80% of my patients choose prayer. Over time, I saw that I was teaching prayer and found that rather silly as a physician. But overall, this is the most proven mind/body effect and is a cornerstone of behavioral medicine."

Dr. Bernie Siegal, founder of the Exceptional Cancer Center in New Haven, Connecticut, tells patients: "Your body knows what's going on in your life. Hope and love prolong life, and despair and hopelessness shorten it."

Now, for a word of personal testimony. No, I'm not throwing away my crutches, since I have none. And I'm not about to grind my trifocals under my heel to prove I don't need them anymore.

I'm just going to confess that for the past six months I've had lower back pains with accompanying pains telegraphing down my right leg. During the same six months I have been under considerable stress.

No, I'm not going to give up the doctor who has been helping me. I'll keep my next appointment!

But I'll tell you what I intend to do — something that at my mellow age I find easy enough to do anyway. I'm going to sit down for about twenty minutes, two times a day, close my eyes, relax, breathe (I still do that quite well) and with each breath exhaled, I'm going to pray a brief breathing-out prayer.

In a few months or so, if you'd like to know, I might tell you, if you should ask, "How's your aching back?"

36. Are Faith in God and Faith in Medicine Incompatible?

Should David and Ginger Twitchell have been found guilty of involuntary manslaughter for trusting God to heal their sick little boy, Robyn, instead of calling for a medical doctor?

The two-and-a-half-year-old child died in 1986 from a bowel obstruction. The trial of the young parents was held in Boston, where Superior Court Judge Sandra Hamlin sentenced the couple to ten years probation when the jury found them guilty.

The Twitchells are young people thoroughly indoctrinated in the Christian Science belief that faith in God and prayer are a valid alternative to generally accepted medical procedures.

They believe this so completely that dependence upon other medical treatment seems contrary, if not inimical, to their belief in spiritual healing.

This is consistent with the classic view of the Christian Science Church that medical treatment and Christian Science intervention are incompatible.

When it was suggested that the case represented an attempt by the majority to impose its morality on the minority, John Kiernan, the special prosecutor, said, "This is not a contest between medicine and religion. Rather it is a marriage of the two. Mainstream America recognizes that prayer and medicine can work well together."

The thinking of honest and sincere Americans will come down on both sides of this issue.

Some will weep for the little boy who was deprived of life almost before it got started, because his parents were so adamant that they would not yield an inch and call in a medical doctor, who might well have saved the child.

"Such people aren't fit to have children!" "Religious bigots!" "Ignorant, stupid people!" "They got what they deserve — only not enough!" All kinds of recriminations come flying through the air.

Others might sympathize with the parents and admire them for their faith. "They had reason to believe little Robyn would be healed through prayer and faith." "There's plenty of well-documented evidence of thousands of people who have been healed without traditional medical assistance."

The judge excluded any such evidence from the case, and would not admit testimony regarding the recognition of Christian Science treatment by health insurance plans.

The Twitchells, no doubt, looked forward to the recovery of

their little boy, and anticipated the reverent joy of telling him one day in the future of his recovery through trust in God and their own loving faith and devoted prayers.

They represent a point of view which has pioneered the way to what promises to be a more complete approach to the healing of human ills.

Some time ago, I referred to a recent conference which was held in Boston on the subject of mind/body medicine. The conference was held under the sponsorship of the University of Massachusetts Medical School and the American Holistic Medical Association.

The conference reported that physicians now know from precise, controlled studies that the body makes specific chemicals in response to thoughts and emotions. These chemicals communicate what a person is thinking and feeling — and believing — to the cells of the body through a network linking brain, heart, blood vessels, stomach, intestines, and the immune system.

This means that faith and prayer are vitally important to healing, and should be regarded with the same respect as recognized medical treatment and procedures.

There's a hint of arrogance in the attitude of any doctor who rejects these spiritual values out of hand. There is no less a hint of arrogance where people of faith reject the benefits of modern medicine and surgery.

My wife and I have a grandson who, as a tiny baby, had a condition like little Robyn's. We all thank God for the dedicated skill of the surgeon who removed the obstruction — while all of us prayed.

Faith should never be a reluctant or unwilling companion in any undertaking to save a human life.

37.   They Just Can't Wait to Die

There's a hot issue brewing. While other topics may be shoved to the back burner to simmer awhile, this one is bound to steam and boil on the front of the range.

It began to heat up when Dr. Jack Kevorkian, a retired pathologist, offered the services of his "death medicine" to 54-year-old Janet Adkins, together with specific instructions.

Debate on the religious and medical ethics of do-it-yourself euthanasia is just beginning. All kinds of reactions are popping and sputtering.

Kevorkian, the suicide "facilitator," one of the first of what may become an entirely new profession of "thanatists," was confronted by Deborah Norville on NBC's "Today" show.

"Some would say you're playing God."

"Well, everybody plays God," replied Kevorkian. "Any intervention into a natural process in the human body is playing God."

Then there's a lot of talk about "dignified death" going around — a concept which may well involve a contradiction of terms.

Also there's the "living will" debate. Such a will is an individual's written and signed request directing doctors and other medical professionals when and under what circumstances life support measures are to be discontinued.

Janet Adkins' suicide was based upon a supposition and a probability. The supposition was that she was a victim of Alzheimer's disease, which gradually robs an individual of memory and other mental faculties.

The tragedy of Mrs. Adkins' final leave-taking is sharpened by the fact that, according to Dr. Vernon Mark, a retired Boston neurosurgeon, 30 percent of Alzheimer's diagnoses are incorrect. The disease cannot be diagnosed with certainty while a person is still alive.

The disease, says Mark, is often mistaken for severe depression or effects of prescription drugs.

The probability, as Mrs. Adkins saw it, was that she — a woman who had climbed Mount Hood and flown a glider, ridden in hot-air balloons, loved music and tennis — would have all these things taken from her.

With all due respect to Mrs. Adkins and her family, it is difficult to avoid the conclusion that she rushed into death as she rushed into life — wanting either a full cup or no cup at all.

The doctor who assisted Mrs. Adkins in her last act was apparently not qualified to determine her mental condition to make sure she was not suffering from a deep depression instead of Alzheimer's disease.

Depressions, which lead to suicidal wishes, and often to actual suicide, are reversible; and many persons who have come through a depression with the help of counseling and psycho-therapy are living today with a newfound zest for life.

It could be said that Janet Adkins loved life, that she was life-accepting and life-affirming. But was it life she affirmed, or merely a fine quality of life which she could not tolerate the thought of losing?

Anyone who has ever counseled with individuals who are severely depressed is aware that the thought of suicide is always near the surface.

The suicidal thought is, "If I can't live the way I want to live, with the values and relationships I enjoy, I don't want to live at all."

If Dr. Kevorkian had been as well trained in dealing with the human soul as he undoubtedly is trained in pathology, he might have been able to detect signs of a typical depression from which this fine woman could have found relief and ongoing life.

There are too many people, young and old, who experience depression for us to conclude that, because anyone wants to die, he or she has the right to die — with medical science assisting.

There is still much to be said for the old-fashioned idea that life is sacred, a gift from God, and that to willfully abandon it is unwise and ungrateful.

38.　　The Hamlet Syndrome

"To be, or not to be . . ." Hamlet has come down from the stage and walks among us.

Suicide has become a rational option. No longer is pressing the self-destruct button considered irrational.

With the emergence of Dr. Jack Kevorkian and his suicide machine, and the accounts of three women whom he has assisted in taking their own lives, we may all be obliged to re-think the subject.

Since Janet Adkins of Portland, Oregon, used the services of Kevorkian in ending her life in June 1990, there have been two other suicides with the "death doctor" assisting.

And now, the door opens wider. *Final Exit,* written by Derek Humphry, founder and executive director of the Hemlock Society, was a sellout, with 41,000 copies of the book in its first printing. It is a how-to-do-it manual, presenting in precise detail the step-by-step procedures for self-destruction.

The subject of suicide was considered of such importance that it was presented as Initiative 119 in the state of Washington on November 5, 1991, where it was defeated, but only after hard work on the part of the Catholic Church and pro-life groups. The issue, unlike Dr. Kevorkian's "patients," is not likely to die.

The reason? It seems that while many people are not afraid to die, they do fear the circumstances which are often the prelude to death: suffering, indignity, dependency, expense, loss of control over one's life, and burdening others.

Underlying the suicide option are certain assumptions and perceptions which need to be carefully examined.

One of these is that there is something almost shamefully wrong about being dependent upon others — even close relatives. But the fact is we are all dependent upon one another, and interdependent with one another. To acknowledge this may be one of the first steps in dealing with life on realistic terms. The interaction of giving and receiving weaves the fabric of human life, from infancy to old age.

To choose death at one's own hand over dependency in illness is the rejection of a vital pattern in human existence. We all need to give and we all need to receive. This is the way we, as humans, function.

Another assumption which enters into the life and death equation is that my life is my own, to do with as I choose. My body is my own. Its pleasures are mine; its pains are mine. If it no longer brings me pleasure, but gives me pain instead, it is my privilege to part with it in my own way at my own time. And nobody should interfere with my decision.

But is my life really my own? Am I its source? Did I make it? Do I sustain its vital processes through the nights and days, the decades? Do I manage its mysterious rhythms? Is it my voice that commands my pulse, the flow of blood, the transformation of nourishment into sight and hearing, flesh and bone?

In all honesty, I can't claim this kind of ownership or management. It's beyond me. It's greater than I am. It's the host; I'm the guest. An invitation was sent and somehow, I responded. Was the response part of the invitation, and from the same source?

Still another assumption is that life's boundaries and meanings are the product of human thought and design.

How far can it reach? What is its worth? What is its purpose? We take our cues from men and women who ultimately know no more than we know about the real meaning of life.

We permit these ideas to box us in until we think success, along with wealth, youth, and power is heaven. Failure, poverty, and weakness are hell. Political, social, and financial influence are the length and breadth of life's meaning.

To think this way is to profane life, to reduce it to a purely secular scheme where nobody finally wins. No mystery, no glory, and no eternal gain.

It seems we have come to the place where we either sanctify life, and see it as a trust from God, or we secularize it, and see it orphaned and alone, without meaning or ultimate purpose.

39.   Reality Calls for Religion

Remember when serious-minded people used to talk about the vast gulf that lay between science and religion? "Never the twain shall meet" and all that.

Well, it seems the gulf is getting narrower, and the twain are not quite so twain.

And it's all happening because there's a planet in danger and some people are becoming concerned about it.

One of these is Professor Charles Birch, an Australian ecologist who was recently awarded what is called religion's "Nobel Prize." Actually, it's the Templeton Prize for Progress in Religion.

Maybe science and religion somehow got together in Birch genetically, since his father was a Methodist minister. Birch himself is a member of the Uniting Church of Australia, a union of Methodist, Congregationalist, and Presbyterian churches.

Let him rock you back on your heels with a salvo of words like this: "There's something wrong about the way we're operating in the world," he says. "To save the planet, people's perceptions of God and creation need to change."

These words have shock value. They may disturb both the scientific community and segments of the religious community.

For a scientist to be talking about God in this way is — well, it's downright "unscientific." And for this maverick biologist and "mere layman" in the field of religion to presume to talk about changing religious folks' perceptions of God — well, that's outright heresy, the kind of thing rewarded in earlier days by the heretic being burned at the stake, with all the "godly" gathered around thanking God that they had been delivered from the hands of Satan.

Whatever may be said about Birch's religious credentials, his scientific ones seem to be in good shape. "He's one of the two or three most distinguished ecologists in the wrold," says ecologist Paul Ehrlich of Stanford University.

Templeton, the founder of the Templeton Prize for Progress in Religion, one of the world's largest cash prizes awarded for anything, along with being one of the globe's most successful financiers, is an active layman in his church.

Like the recipient of the award, Templeton says he sees something more than a mere "linkage" between the spiritual and material facets of life. "The spiritual aspect is the totality of one's life," he says. "The material benefits which come to a genuinely spiritual person are not the reason for one's being spiritually-oriented, they are the consequences."

So, two worlds, long considered alien to each other — the economic and the spiritual — are coming together in men like Birch and Templeton. Is it too soon to say, "Hail to the men of a new age and a better world"?

Birch says modern science is beginning to realize it can't reproduce our world with a building-block model. "There's something mental in existence," he says, "which we let slip through our fingers... From protons to people, you have to look at them more as subjects rather than objects. Then you can see much more easily the relationship of God — not just to human beings, but to all of creation ... God can be incarnate in life, but cannot be incarnate in machinery."

Birch says God isn't a mechanic tinkering with wheels and cogs and gears, He's "persuasive love. Love that persuades creation to become what it can be." There's power in love says this scientist, "and in the end, the only power that matters is love."

He sees love as respect for life and reverence for creation —the only force sufficient to save a threatened planet that has been raped by men devoid of this kind of love.

What was it they used to say about science and religion being "worlds apart"? Maybe what made it seem so was that men and their real world were worlds apart.

Reality calls for penitence for savaging this lovely little planet that is less like a machine and more like a poem and a prayer. Reality calls for religion.

40.   Love — On the Battlefield?

Did I dream it in one of my nod-offs while listening to the flow of war news gushing from the pipes of CNN, or did I really hear it?

There was this marine officer somewhere in Saudi Arabia, being interviewed about the morale of his troops. What I heard sounded like the audio track had slipped out of sync with the picture on the screen and got mixed up with some TV preacher's sermon.

What the marine leader said, or what I heard him say, is that the most important force in keeping his unit in shape for whatever happens — come hell or high water — is love. I still have trouble believing I heard this.

These tough young American warriors, lean and mean from constant training and discipline, were being taught what some of them may have learned in Sunday School back in some little village church, but never took seriously. Here in the restless sands of the Middle East they were hearing it all over again —not just to make them "good boys," but to keep them alive when the going got rough.

As I recall, it was Captain John Admire who was talking about love and survival. I heard him use the word again in another interview when he said, "I have too much love for those boys to send them in before everything's ready."

Just to make sure I hadn't been dreaming or that I was not projecting a spiritual value inappropriately into a military situation, I got on the phone with the nearest marine I could find. It happened to be Gunnery Sergeant Wayne Jackson at the marine recruiting station in the Blue Hen Mall in Dover, Delaware.

"Did I hear it right?" I asked Jackson.

The marine seemed a little hesitant at first to use the word *love*. He talked all around it, but finally got down to it.

Edging into the subject, he began to read from a document known as "The Bond of Brothers Code" of the United States Marines.

Soon I was hearing expressions like "dignity and respect . . . coming to the aid of a buddy . . . each person fully belongs, is fully accepted by those he eats with, fights with, and may die with . . . Share your eyes with each other and so learn to see things from a different angle . . . blending of cultures . . . take care of each other . . .”

The marine sergeant told me it's important to get to know the guy who might be next to you in a foxhole under fire. Getting to know why he's the way he is, and respecting him for whatever makes him different from you — which means accepting him for himself and not somebody else.

“What would happen if we turned this ‘Bond of Brothers Code’ head over heels and imagined that instead of trust and mutual acceptance and respect, there were suspicion, distrust, and rejection of the other guy because he happened to have a different color or creed or came from a different cultural background?”

“It would ruin the whole thing,” he said. “The Marine Corps would fall apart.” They wouldn't need any outside enemy to defeat them, they would go down from lack of the one thing that holds them together in war and peace — a practical, honest, tough love for one another.

A passing thought buzzed by me. If this kind of bonding could be achieved in other groups of human beings in normal times, there might be no need for wars like the one that was going on “over there.”

We need respect for people as people, however different they are from us or anybody we ever knew. Acceptance of everyone as belonging to the same love-disciplined family. Coming to one another's help in times of need. It is important that you have the feeling you are not alone in a hostile world, but have the backing and support of the guy next to you. What an atmosphere for the work place, home place, the place of worship.

I never thought I would hear it from a marine officer surrounded by toughened, ready-for-anything marines — this word that so many hesitate to say. But there it was on the lips of an honest-to-goodness marine officer, and in “The Bond of Brothers Code” — something that keeps saying “love never fails.”

41.   The Strange Uses of Religion

Religion was going off all over the place like anti-aircraft fire in the night skies above Iraq and Saudi Arabia. Everybody with any kind of religious point of view, however bizarre, was popping off.

Saddam Hussein, a shameless secularist who nevertheless knows how to use religion for his own purposes, was offering unabashed photo opportunities showing himself prostrate on his prayer rug.

The hypocrisy of his ersatz piety was transparent to all except some devout Muslims who wanted to believe that their leader, like themselves, was a true believer. The symbol, however empty, was meant to give them courage to continue their struggle, even to death.

On "our side," as American military persons in Saudi Arabia packed their military gear to move up to the "front," Bibles and New Testaments were carefully stowed.

From the beginning of Desert Storm, Baghdad radio had been beaming select passages from the *Koran*, Islam's holy book, in the hope of raising the conflict to the level of a holy war.

On this side again, Hal Lindsey's once popular book, *The Late Great Planet Earth*, which prophesies the Battle of Armageddon, Earth's last great battle in which evil will be conquered, was realizing a renewed popularity. So had another book dealing with the same theme, *Armageddon, Oil, and the Middle East Crisis* by John F. Walvoord.

Churches across the United States reported larger than usual congregations on the Sunday preceding the war's outbreak. In the Middle East, 550 chaplains were attempting to minister to the spiritual needs of the troops.

"Foxhole religion is quite valid" among the service personnel, reported Captain James O'Connor, chief chaplain aboard the aircraft carrier USS John F. Kennedy. He said chapel attendance on his ship had increased 40%.

Jewish War Veterans of America, concerned about the religious life of their sons and daughters in uniform, raised money for a special printing of pocket-size Bibles for Jewish troops, waiting in the Saudi sands with Christian and Muslin warriors for the zero hour.

In Washington, as tense hours edged toward the January 15 deadline, there was a flurry of religious activity in the White House.

As the critical hour neared, President George Bush got on the phone with Presiding Bishop Edmon Browning of the Episcopal Church, and United States Senate Chaplain, Richard Halverson, and told them he was praying for peace. Both clergymen prayed with the President on the phone. Bishop Browning urged him to seek a peaceful solution, adding that two wrongs never make a right.

On Wednesday, January 16, Bush sent an urgent call to a long-time friend, Billy Graham, saying "I need you." Graham arrived at the White House about 5:45 p.m. Unknown to him, allied planes were already airborne and on their way to Baghdad.

"Now you know," said Barbara Bush to Graham when the news broke on TV that evening. During the night the evangelist prayed with Bush and others.

The President, it seemed, found more comfort with Billy Graham, who has been overnight guest twice at the White House since war began, than with Bishop Browning.

The uses of religion in times of war often seem strange and numerous. Some use it to get divine guidance on decisions already made. For some it is a lens through which they contemplate the end of the world. Many use it to whip up hatred against evil — which is always on "the other side." Some use it to dub a war as "just."

An appropriate use of religion and prayer in such times might embrace some measure of penitence and sorrow. It is tragic that, after all these years, we human beings who occupy the planet Earth have to resort to killing one another with the most sophisticated means human intelligence can devise.

42.   When Reality Breaks In —
Suddenly, We Are Religious

The few weeks following January 15, 1991, would witness a return of people to the churches and synagogues throughout America. People who were rarely seen in the soft light of stained-glass windows would be seen there.

Why and how come? There was a war going on in the Middle East, which reached into all our lives. War has a way of stripping us of many of the popular illusions which draw us away from our deepest religious values.

When the illusions vanish, we find ourselves reaching out for what we call God. Take those young airmen from the army's 82nd Airborne Division of Fort Bragg, North Carolina, quartered somewhere in Saudi Arabia.

Jeff Houston, the unit's chaplain, said, "This is more like a revival than a war . . . We have four worship services each and every day . . . averaging over 160 . . . Last Sunday we had 12 professions of faith; the Sunday before we had 18."

War confronts us with realities which we lose sight of amid the pleasant illusions of everyday life. When we're obliged to face these realities, we reach out for something beyond ourselves and our own resources.

It's not merely that we want God on our side; it's something deeper — the cry of the human soul standing naked, stripped of all its comfortable illusions that life goes on and on, and tomorrow will come, and we're in complete control of our lives.

It's the birthright of the young to think they are invulnerable — a warm reassuring thought when you're young. Death is a reality for old people only, those who have lived their lives.

But those young men in Saudi Arabia could no longer wrap themselves in this comforter. So they reached out to God with whatever faith they could find in themselves and one another.

For some, it came in the form of a prayer for help. For some, a kind of penitent apology like, "Sorry, God, but I've overlooked you. Please don't overlook me!" For others, it was an affirmation that there is something greater than all that is going on or will ever go on — something greater than anything that can ever happen.

Crises such as war reveal us to ourselves as we are, with all our bravado pretenses and comfortable assumptions swept aside.

We're scared, angry, frustrated, lonely, heartbroken, self-doubting like that 23-year-old airman who streaked over Iraq's Republican Guard and dropped his first rack of bombs on what he realized were men like himself, with families and friends at home hoping and praying for their safe return.

The young man appeared shocked, haunted, even guilty, despite the fact that he had done precisely what he was supposed to do. Confused that what was so wrong could be so right, what was so right as to receive the applause of the ground crew could be so wrong.

We're uncomfortable, confused, and even resentful when reality breaks into our smug little world of make-believe — like the football fan criticizing the heightened security arrangements for the Super Bowl game in Tampa. "I don't want the real world to interfere with my little world," he said, like a petulant child called away from his play to take care of unfinished chores.

When we have our games, when we feel sure we'll see tomorrow's sun, and when we are in confident control of our lives, we're sure we don't need anything beyond ourselves. But when reality comes crashing in and all our symbols of security tremble, when all our comfortable illusions evaporate, we do what human beings in all ages have done — we call upon God.

43.   We Can't Honor God With a Lie

Days of thanksgiving — April 5-7, 1991. In response to President George Bush's proclamation setting those days aside for this purpose, church bells rang and the national flag snapped in the breeze from thousands of staffs. A time of rejoicing.

Dared anyone suggest that the happy mood of celebration be sombered a bit to allow for mourning? Those days in April were "a time to mourn" in Iraq, and a decent respect for their dead and ours, resulting from the Desert Storm conflict, might have moved us to join them in their grief.

"That's their problem!" a cocky chauvinistic attitude might compel us to say. Of course it is, but to the extent that we're all human beings living in the same world, it's ours as well. In another sense that brings it closer to home, it's ours as well as theirs, since our hundred died with their hundred thousand — all dead before their lives had barely begun.

There was a blind-sidedness to the presidential proclamation unless its few spare words expressing condolence "for all those who made the ultimate sacrifice" carried more of a burden of sincere mourning than they seemed to carry.

Lying in the sands of the Middle East are the bodies of over 100,000 young Iraqis who were first the victims of their own leadership, then victims of our arms. Like some of our own young people who bade good-bye to mates and sweethearts, little babies and old friends in the hope of returning home, they disappeared into the sands.

Through the mourning eyes of our own, we reach out empty arms for a young American military man or woman who will never come home. Mourning would have become us as we shed a tear for the people of Iraq in those days of their mourning.

There have been reiterated reminders by our president, and others in high positions, that we have nothing against the people of Iraq. This would have been a good time to flesh out these statements through sharing their mourning as we expressed our own.

Nothing could have won the hearts of many ordinary people of Iraq more than for us to have let them know that in our season of thanksgiving, we were also mourning — for our fallen and for theirs.

Unless we let our rejoicing in victory have its full measure of mourning and humility, we might find ourselves distorting values which we are sure to need both sooner and later, as we pursue our national destiny.

There is something of hypocrisy in the words of the proclamation, "The Lord gives victory 'not by might, nor by power...'"

Honesty and respect for God oblige us to face the fact, known and accepted throughout the world, that it was by "might (and) by power" of superior arms that the war was won. We cannot honor God with a patent lie. If we want to recognize Him, let it be within the context of truth.

The President's proclamation begins with a quote from an ancient Psalm: "O give thanks to the Lord for He is gracious, for His mercy endures forever."

Look at the killing fields where young men and women fell in death, and ask what kind of merciful God can be thanked for that.

In our sincere gratitude and desire to reverence God, we need to be careful that we do not blemish humanity's faith in a God of mercy and compassion. We desperately need to hold to that pure faith — "keep it holy."

Theology has traveled a long, rocky road to raise human faith in God from narrow tribal concepts to a universal Fatherhood. Let us be careful that we don't let it slip back — especially in a time when a shrinking world calls for wider thoughts.

Another quote from sacred scriptures in the President's proclamation was "Come behold the works of the Lord . . . He makes wars to cease to the end of the earth." Good words, words full of hope. But one can't help but wonder if they would not have been more appropriate as part of a different document. One which, instead of blessing a devastating war, had followed a successful effort to win peace through peaceful means. This is the kind of thing millions of people throughout the world prayed for.

Let the bells ring! Let the bells toll.

44.   A War Won — A Peace Lost?

Did you hear what General Norman Schwartzcopf said to the staff of officers accompanying him as he lumbered through the sand toward the official tent in Safwan where Iraqi officers were to meet them for what amounted to surrender ceremonies ending the Gulf War?

He must have known he was on TV and that his words would echo around the world. "We don't want them to be embarrassed . . .

humiliated," he said in a kind of stage whisper.

Was this the same man under whose command tons of bombs rained from the skies on the enemy just days before?

Was this the "bear," "Stormin' Norman," the man who wouldn't give an inch while the fight was still on and the guns of war were still thundering?

Now the guns were silent. This was a different time, a time for peacemaking. Still in his military camouflage, the burly general knew all too well that how a peace is made determines whether a war is really won.

This is a lesson dearly learned. When Germany was defeated in World War I, President Woodrow Wilson pleaded with the other allies to accept reasonable terms for peace, leaving the German people with room for self-respect and a reasonable measure of dignity.

With this, the arrogant Georges Clemenceau of France barked back, "You talk like Jesus Christ!" In the French premier's mind this translated into "impractical."

When Clemenceau's harsh attitude prevailed, and punitive conditions were imposed upon Germany, the world thought the Great War was over. But not long after the Treaty of Versailles was signed, an embittered German war veteran by the name of Adolph Hitler caught the attention of a humiliated, defeated nation, and World War II was firing its guns.

Following that war, General Douglas Mac Arthur as Supreme Commander insisted that Japan not be humiliated by the conquerors which he had led in battle, though many shrill voices clamored for just that. His philosophy prevailed, and a lasting peace between Japan and the United States resulted.

All of which adds up to the conclusion that we have arrived at another time in history when we need to shelve our military manuals and unroll the Sermon on the Mount — not merely to be pious, but to be practical, and to save human lives in time to come.

The ancient words heard originally on a rolling green hillside overlooking the Sea of Galilee take on contemporary significance as we hear them now.

"Blessed are those who mourn . . ."

President George Bush said recently he cannot completely

join the euphoria over victory in the Persian Gulf. This becomes him. We can be happy that our troops are home, and that the war is over. But, when we reflect on the tragedy of more than 100,000 young lives wasted in a few days, mourning becomes us.

"Blessed are those who hunger and thirst for righteousness…" Righteousness means what is right, not merely what may serve national interests at the moment, but what is both just and fair. The end of this war gives us one more opportunity to try to make things right in the Middle East — including making room in the land once called Palestine for its historic inhabitants, the Palestinians.

"Blessed are the merciful, for they shall obtain mercy . . ." Only a victor with the capacity to plant his boot on the neck of a fallen foe can know what mercy is. Our great country has one more chance to show mercy — and obtain mercy for the world.

"Blessed are the peacemakers . . ." If we, as a nation, were prepared to invest a fraction of the brainpower and money into making peace as we have invested in the Gulf War, we would be well on the way to the realization of the dreams and prayers of many generations!

This may be the time to enlist the best brains of the United States and the rest of the world in a study of peace — and to place that study on as high a level as the study of war.

45.   Shalom . . . Salaam

"Blessed are the peacemakers," said Kamel Abu-Jaber, Jordon's Foreign Minister, at the opening of the historic peace conference between Israel and the Arab nations of the Middle East, convened in Madrid, Spain.

"Shalom," said Israel's Prime Minister, Yitzhak Shamir, as he began his address before the assemblage gathered around the T-shaped table formation.

Each man was echoing the words of another man as he stood in the rolling green hills of Galilee nearly 2,000 years ago.

Never before has the word *peace* cut through such hostility, suspicion, and bitterness as the fog of mutual hatred hanging over those tables.

Up to this point, the peace-seeking adversaries had not as much as shaken hands. They had not even permitted themselves direct eye contact.

Preaching to the other side, justifying their own position, denying the other's position. So went one of the most critical gatherings ever assembled.

Something has to break through if good is to come of the peace conference that gathered under the fresco of Greek gods.

Not that substituting one fresco or wall hanging for another would accomplish much good, but it might be worth the try. Take those words of the Sermon on the Mount, quoted by Kamel Abu-Jaber, and echoed by Yitzhak Shamir and let them dominate the room — in Madrid or wherever the adversaries may agree to meet again.

Peace is not something in and of itself. It is the result of changes and adjustments which must take place in the minds of human beings whose maladjustments break out into hostility.

"Blessed are the pure in spirit . . ." These are the happily-adjusted people who have faced the fact that without values which money cannot buy, they're poor. To such people belongs the bright heaven-on-earth, which others miss in their desperate struggles for wealth and land — and power.

"Blessed are they that mourn . . ." People who feel this way can afford to shed a few tears over a raped and savaged Earth. Here, human lives are lost in striving for values which turn to ashes once they are won.

"Blessed are the meek . . ." The meek, the teachable, men and women and nations are willing to learn the lessons of history and experience. Unless we human beings are willing to sit down and learn from what has been, we might shudder at what will be.

"Blessed are those who hunger and thirst after righteousness . . ." These people want to see right prevail, not merely what is expedient or what serves their purpose at the moment.

"Blessed are the merciful . . ." Merciful people are those who take a step beyond fairness and justice and move to compassion for others over whom, at the moment, they may have some edge of authority or power.

"Blessed are the pure in heart . . ." Sincere people, un-hypocritical people, are what they seem to be; not given to deception, subterfuge, and insincerity in order to win friends and influence people.

It's interesting to note that, in His Sermon on the Mount, Jesus of Nazareth did not come to the subject of peace until He had discussed those other things, as though He knew and wanted to remind others that peace is the fruit which grows on these branches. Without the vine and without the branches, no grapes.

The Israeli and Arab peace-seekers will assemble in other places during what may well be a long and feverish struggle. Tempers will flare and whispers will become shouts. But wherever they assemble, wherever they debate, it would do no harm to hang the complete text of the Sermon on the Mount where all can see it and contemplate its historic and contemporary meaning.

46. The Gentle Divorce

After shopkeepers, florists, and the rest of us have done our annual bit to help Anna May Jarvis commemorate her mother's death in May 1905 by dutifully celebrating Mother's Day, I begin to feel a little queasy.

Not that I'm against motherhood — heaven forbid! It's just a feeling that I've participated in making too much of a good thing — like the time I bought a bag of coconut as a kid and ate it all on the way home.

Coconut was so good on top of a cake; and the idea of having a whole bag of it all to myself was something out of this world —where I almost ended up. I spent the rest of the day with a horrible bellyache and nausea.

Motherhood, like coconut, is a good thing — in its place. And it definitely has a place, but it's not the whole cake. It's part of a recipe that calls for other ingredients in proper measures.

I've often wondered if Anna May Jarvis had a father. She must have had — since without one her dear mother could never have become her dear mother; and dear Anna May could never have become Anna May. Did she ever think of honoring him, I wonder?

There's something wrong about making so much over one part of a vital duo and so little of the other part. And women receiving all that adulation heaped on them once a year with glowing Mother's Day sermons, corsages, rings, pins, necklaces, and such, must feel just a little guilty when they realize their honored position is supported by a less honored one.

Yes, I mean fatherhood. Not just because I'm a father, but because I had a father — and so did all the other kids in the neighborhood. Sometimes he was much less visible than mother, and in some cases, the kids didn't even know who he was — although there were stories about him.

But in most cases he was just as visible as mother. He was a young, hard-working provider and protector of his family. And we all looked forward to his coming home from work with half a sandwich that he had left for one of us in his lunch box.

Now how did these two people ever get separated from each other by five weeks — each with a different day to celebrate their importance to each other and to us?

Mother's Day, the second Sunday in May. Father's Day, the third Sunday in June. They were married on the same day, listening to those words: "What therefore God hath joined together, let not man put asunder."

The minister forgot to include kids in that "asunder" phrase. And here we are putting apart those whom God joined together — we, their kids, separating them like they didn't even belong to each other.

Frankly, I don't like it. And I've made up my mind — as a clergyman, father, lover of mother and father, and the whole family — that I'm not going along with this ceremonial divorce another year.

What's wrong with having a Family Day? If shopkeepers and florists and other beneficiaries of the dual celebrations should feel threatened by this arrangement, they could still sell their stuff — a corsage for mom, a necktie for dad. And maybe some things for the kids — because they're part of the family too.

In our brave new world of gadgets and gimmicks and things, there are too many forces pulling the family apart. Husbands and fathers go one way. Wives and mothers another way. And the kids go a dozen different other ways.

We sure don't need special days to separate them still further. So, Mr. Chairman, or Ms. Chairperson, whoever you are and wherever you are, I move, Sir, Ma'am, that in the interest of family unity and all those precious things preachers preach about on Mother's Day and Father's Day, that we have a marriage of the two days and call it Family Day.

The day shall include recognition of all mothers, all fathers, all children. And on that day let us all celebrate the goodness of life together!

47. The Glue That Makes Marriages Stick

What's the glue that holds marriages together? Sex? Money? Better houses? More conveniences? Cars? Sit back. Take a deep breath. Would you believe religion?

A recent study by Marianne E. Ferber of the University of Illinois and William Sander of De Paul University, both economists, looking for an economic answer, came up with — of all things — a religious one.

Their study showed that there is a close correlation between "going to the altar," staying near the altar, and having marriages that last.

Divorce rates are lowest in states where church membership is highest, and highest where church membership is lowest, according to the study.

Five states with soaring divorce rates — Nevada, Oregon, Florida, Alaska, and Arizona, register the lowest percentage of their population who are members of churches and synagogues.

Five states with the highest church membership — Utah, North Dakota, Rhode Island, South Dakota, and Wisconsin —

have the lowest divorce rates.

William D. Brown, a clinical psychologist and marriage counselor who has his practice in Washington, D. C., says, "Those who are religiously oriented have a substantial advantage in keeping their marriage together over people who do not have that type of base."

Well, I've always suspected that religion makes a difference in avoiding the divorce court.

But let's not go too fast here. Let's not crowd the altars with people who want to take out church membership as a kind of insurance to save their marriages.

No one would guarantee that just by joining a church or synagogue or mosque, a couple will maintain their marital union. No more than standing at the altar saying "I will" in response to the ritual questions of the marriage ceremony.

So what's the religious orientation or content that makes a difference between a failed marriage and a fulfilled one?

Dorothy Savage, executive director of the Commission on Family Ministries and Human Sexuality for the National Council of Churches, concluded that the study "bears out the belief that religion counterbalances society's continued emphasis on self."

Elaborating on this point, Savage says further, "Religion in all its forms tells the individual that service, sacrificing oneself and going the extra mile are of value, and coincidentally are the kind of things that help a marriage work."

In reaching this conclusion, she put her finger down on what may well be the most significant effect of religion upon human behavior — the sublimation of ego, the handling of self.

All of the great religions deal with the problem of self in relation to others.

Marriage is a relationship between two individuals, each with a natural, or unnatural sense of self-importance. Like sovereign states entering into a union, each individual entering into marriage needs to be able and willing to surrender some element of sovereign independence if the union is to be successful.

Unless each of the marital partners makes a sacrifice of his or her will, desire, ambition, and independence upon the altar of their union, sooner or later one part of the union is going to secede, and there goes the union!

Everything in the marriage will become a point of conflict and contest between two egos: sex, money, house, relatives, car, and children . . .

With some measure of ego reduction, through reasonable "self-denial," all of these become areas of mutual sharing, enjoyment, and fulfillment.

48. Marital Vagrancy and Worn-Out Marriages

It's June. John and Mary stand before the altar. Mary is pretty in her white lace bride's gown. John is handsome in his rented tuxedo.

Bridesmaids are nervously in place. The best man and ushers flank the groom. The minister intones the ritual question. John says "I will." Mary says "I will."

Then the solemn iambics, "for better, for worse, for richer, for poorer, in sickness and in health, to love and to cherish, 'til death us do part."

Those brave, lovely words. As a clergyman I've coached hundreds of couples to say them. There's an inescapable sadness in the realization that half of them may have ended on the rocks with the national percentages.

Even where the marriages somehow held together, some didn't remember to "forsake all other." What God had joined together they let man — or woman — put asunder.

A recent survey by *USA Today* reveals that even in reasonably successful marriages 63% of the grooms have cheated on their brides, and 37% of the brides have cheated.

With figures like these in mind, Mary Ann Bartusis, author of "Every Other Man," has worked up a vulnerability chart, calling attention to points of weakness which might lead to marital cheating.

Fifteen questions, provided with yes and no boxes, running the gamut from family history of physical or sexual abuse, through tolerance of a partner's idiosyncrasies, omit even the slightest reference to those marriage vows so sweetly spoken on that beautiful June day.

Maybe the failed and failing couples missed the point of what they were saying and doing as they stood in the soft light falling through stained-glass windows.

Something, grandly implied, missed them in the excitement of the ceremony and the reception that followed, with Mary cutting a piece of the wedding cake and feeding it to John, while all the cameras flashed.

There was one strong, compelling reason why they wanted their wedding ceremony held in church and not a magistrate's court or in the bride's parents' beautiful garden by the river.

Something "reverent," they say, "more appropriate." The words they feel but can't frame have to do with a sacred tradition which embraces marriage as bride and groom embrace each other when the minister pronounces them "husband and wife together."

The altar. The soft music. The stained-glass windows. The sacred place. These have always been important in the significant moments of life.

The place, the symbols, the words, conspire to make a statement: "Life comes from beyond itself. Its beginning, its ending, and all in between are pure gift. Accept it as a gift from life's Eternal Source, or else never really experience it."

For one high moment in their lives, those two people before the altar acknowledged this. The sacred ritual, the reverent ambiance, said it for them — the confession that neither, though deeply in love, could satisfy the deepest needs of the other.

If each expects supreme happiness from the other, they're in for disappointment. If their disappointment throws them into other arms, more disappointment.

To expect "the drink divine" from a human cup places more strain on human relationships than they were ever meant to bear.

If John and Mary can't find happiness within themselves through a grateful acceptance of their lives as God's gift to them, they will lean too heavily upon each other and wear their love thin.

Marital vagrants who hop from bed to bed looking for satisfaction probably are not overly-sexed or erotically hyper so much as they are individuals who have never accepted themselves and consequently can't accept anyone else or be accepted by anyone else.

49.   Sex Is Good, But . . .

When science comes down on the side of traditional morality and the church comes down on the side of immorality, things begin to seem a little crazy out there.

In the Presbyterian Church (U.S.A.) a committee of seventeen ministers, academics, and health professionals published a report calling for the church to withdraw its support from Biblical morality in favor of something more "user friendly."

Traditionally the Presbyterian Church (U.S.A.), like many other churches, has maintained a moral stance which strongly encouraged sexual abstinence before marriage, fidelity within marriage, and chastity afterward.

The report under the title "Keeping Body and Soul Together" called for a relaxation of traditional morality, and approving sexual gratification outside as well as inside marriage.

Calling it "justice-love" the report seems to regard sexual gratification — regardless of how it is achieved, or with whom, or how many — as the *summum bonum,* the greatest good to be experienced by a human being — and no one should be denied it, whether single, married, young or old, heterosexual or homosexual.

In contrast with this laid-back, casual morality proposed under the aegis of the church, consider the severe, straight-laced morality of Dr. Robert C. Noble of the University of Kentucky College of Medicine, quoted in the May 6, 1991 issue of *Newsweek.*

Noble is an infectious-disease physican who specializes in AIDS treatment for the poor. From this position, addressing the subject of AIDS, Noble says, "Nobody these days lobbies for abstinence, virginity, or single lifetime sexual partners. That would be boring."

Then he quotes from a recent government report: "Abstinence and sexual intercourse with one mutually faithful uninfected partner are the only totally effective prevention strategies." Sounds sort of like, "Thou shall not commit adultery." Doesn't it?

Wouldn't it be too bad if just when a strong morality is needed, with such clear reasons for it so evident, that the church should turn its back upon a morality which has helped keep the human race alive?

We modern people need to be careful how we dispose of commandments. "Thou shalt not covet thy neighbor's wife . . . Thou shalt not commit adultery . . ." These are ancient commandments, but apparently whoever talked with Moses up there on the mountain amid the rolling thunder seemed to know what works and what doesn't work for human beings.

I've read a story somewhere of a liberal missionary who went to a tribe of former cannibals. While conversing with the chief, the missionary said cavalierly, "We modern people don't pay much attention to the Bible any more."

The chief's eyes widened as he said, "It's good for you that we take it seriously, my friend, or you might be boiling in a pot right now."

Morality is a way to control strong urges which, if not controlled, would get out of hand. The urges may not be wrong in themselves; actually they may be good — like a fire on a cold night is good; every household from a tent to a mansion needs one.

But unless the cozy little fire is controlled, it could burn the place down, together with the entire village or city.

That's why we have fire departments — not to discourage having a fire in your fireplace on a chilly night, or in a cook stove, but to keep the fire within controllable limits.

Sex is good. Without it there would be no family life, no ongoing generations, just a lifeless planet spinning vacant and lonely through space.

But, although it is good, and the urge is strong, it needs to be controlled. Religion has been one of the historical controls, encouraging, even solemnizing, the relationship through marriage.

We don't need to hold to a morality just because it has ancient sources, but we should honor it, if it honors us.

50. The Only Safe Sex
Is Saved Sex

What makes sex the most fascinating, confusing, attractive, repulsive, exciting, delightful, and frightening subject in 20th-century America?

Could it be that it once belonged to a larger picture, and somehow got separated from what gave it meaning, purpose, and direction? Shades of Madonna, Wilt Chamberlin, and "Magic" Johnson.

Is sex like an actor who finds himself alone on the stage without any other members of the cast to give him support, and so has to become the whole show? The lone source of all the desire, humor, tenderness, violence, meant to be shared by other actors.

However it happened, it has happened. Sex has become the focus of human hopes, desires, fears, frustrations, pride, and shame. It is the center from which every other value and relationship, good, bad, and indifferent, derives its significance.

It has been prostituted to sell cars, cigarettes, TVs, VCRs, toothpaste, and denim jeans. According to Tom Brokaw's evening news show on November 18, 1991, even Madison Avenue, aware that sex has been overused, is becoming professionally repentant of too many sexy, sultry, feminine forms draped over shiny new cars, too many cordless phones, exercise machines, and bottles of Scotch, hinting at sensuous pleasures beyond the products themselves.

This overworking of sex to satisfy all of the thirsts of body, mind, and soul has been too much for it to take. So now, drained of its beauty, it comes limping back to us — bent, bruised, raped, and dying of AIDS.

It must sadden anyone who truly cares for young life that the best our wisest "wise men" can offer an emerging generation of young Americans is for schools to dispense condoms along with schoolbooks — under the socially righteous and high-minded notion of promoting "safe sex."

Most everybody knows, or at least suspects, that this is like bailing out a sinking boat with a thimble — or like punching a hole in the boat's bottom to let the water out.

The only "safe sex" is saved sex — saved from its alienation from the rest of life, restored to the warm embrace of love, faith, respect, meaning — and God.

Sex has been running on the wild side, a prodigal male/female lost kid, spending his/her substance in riotous living, dimly remembering a home where all was better once upon a time.

"Home" for sex is where it is safe, because it is saved — saved from alienation from all that gives it real satisfaction and fulfillment. "Home" is where sex is welcomed back and reconciled to its vital relationships.

I witnessed beautiful sex recently. A young man and woman with two adorable children between them. Sexual attraction is not something in and of itself; it is Eternal Wisdom's way of drawing male and female together to replenish and sustain life on a planet, trailing through space, past other planets where life has never found rootage.

As Sam Keen (no known relative of mine) says in his latest book, *Fire In the Belly:* "Sexuality is wonderful . . ., because it is our link with the creative power of being itself. If ever we lose sight of the . . . triad of man-woman-child, we neglect something of the meaning of sexuality."

So, Bruce Willis, who has played the devil-may-care playboy role, finds happiness and meaning for his and his wife's sexuality as he holds their little girl in his arms, and confesses that he has discovered a new spiritual dimension in his life.

This is not, by any means or interpretation, to say that all sex must be for the purpose of procreation. But in whatever pleasure it brings there ought always be the understanding, between male and female, that all sexual acts have consequences beyond the acts themselves.

51. A Playboy Becomes a Spiritual Man

Bruce Willis. Spiritual.

The words don't fit. It's like saying John McEnroe is a great football player or Joe Montana is a whiz with a tennis racquet, or the devil wears a lovely pink halo.

Bruce Willis, who as cool guy David Addison in "Moonlighting," regaled TV audiences for two years with his bad-boy, devil-may-care antics. Spiritual?

This was the shocker that rocked Ann Trebbe of *USA Today* when she interviewed the local boy from Penns Grove, New Jersey, recently.

She probably anticipated a wisecracking routine from Willis, who had let his hair grow and put on thirty pounds for his role in "In Country," a movie that features him as a traumatized Vietnam veteran.

The interviewer couldn't have been ready for what she listened to in the hour-long interview. The playboy of the tabloids talking about responsibility, racism — and of all things, spirituality!

Allow that Willis was never an exact mirror image of David Addison, there was enough of one in the other for Willis to get his kicks out of nights of bar-hopping, greeting the first pink wisps of a new day with bleary eyes.

Maybe he was just tired, too tired, during the interview to be his usual jaunty madcap self. But it wasn't just fatique. It was something else, hinted at early on, then given a name as the interview progressed.

"A more spiritual time in my life" is the way he spoke of the two years since he married Debbi Moore, and fathered their little girl, Rumer.

There was no pious God talk or any religious buzz words, and frankly, I'm glad there wasn't. The spareness of the language hinted at more that could be said but meant more by being left unsaid. Did the interviewer get the feeling at times that this man was on the edge of something too great for mere words, too lovely to be soiled by awkward verbal footprints?

"Spiritual" was the only word he ventured. But maybe I was

hearing the word as conveying more than was ever intended. It might possibly mean no more to Bruce Willis than a new fascination with some soft-spoken, dark-eyed, Indian guru who left his cave in the Himalayas to come to America to satisfy spiritual hunger for a good price.

But there was a reference in the interview to something more profoundly intimate. Something in the way he linked his "more spiritual time" with Rumer, his little one-year-old daughter.

He confessed to the interviewer that the child partly explains the new spiritual dimension of his life. "Everything else is stupid compared to having kids," he said.

Well, I thought, that kind of tender anchorage doesn't leave too much free rope to float around in the murky waters of the wierdly occult. Not much room to go tailing after some mumbo-jumbo wagon with Shirley MacLaine and company.

"A little child shall lead them." A child-led spirituality could be the nearest thing to sanity that many moderns will ever find. Hold up on the Amens! Just let Bruce Willis nod silently, holding his baby girl in his arms.

There is nothing quite as effective in restoring balance to human minds as a little child to play with and love for dear life.

With our modern frenetic preoccupation with orgiastic sex, we have overlooked the obvious value of sexual pleasure to seduce us to the greater pleasure of holding our own child in our arms and seeing one transported moment nine months earlier reflected in the face of a little child.

To playboys and playgirls, Bruce Willis might give a bit of advice from a former playboy: "You're playing around too long at the playground entrance. Come on in and play with a child!"

Where's the old Bruce Willis? In a way, I miss him — or his TV counterpart, wisecracking David Addison. But when I hear about this new "more spiritual" guy, it's better than a fair trade.

          # Life Is Not a Snapshot

At the risk of seeming politically naive, which I may be, and sentimental, which I am, and given to looking for diamonds in garbage, which I do, I want to take my turn at saying something about the recent United States Senate hearings on the nomination of Judge Clarence Thomas to the Supreme Court.

There was one high moment when Senator Joe Biden, chairman of the Judiciary Committee, looked the embattled nominee in the eye and said something which seemed to have originated on a level above all that was going on around the green-covered tables.

Debate and questioning had sunk to the lowest imaginable nadir. Accusations and counter accusations were freely flowing, and expose had reached the cringing point. Tempers were flaring. Thomas registered outrage, anger, and hurt. He confessed that, for him, life seemed to have stopped. A good reputation, he said, had been besmirched, a good name damaged beyond repair.

Biden, who — despite his political leanings — had been conducting a fair hearing, from his position behind the long table, flanked by other senators and staff members, in an earnest voice said to Thomas, "Judge, life is not a snapshot; it's a motion picture."

To some it may have come across as a pious palliative to a man in despair, an empty platitude to one who felt himself sinking in quicksand.

Paul Greenberg, in his column in the October 16 edition of *News Journal,* Wilmington, Delaware, saw it that way and wrote: "In not very subtle references, Biden kept comparing Judge Thomas's ordeal-by-suspicion with his own brushes with plagiarism over the years. Biden acted as if the publicity engendered by his problems with attribution were comparable with having uncorroborated accusations of the vilest behavior paraded before the entire, television-addicted country day after day, night after night — prime time and replays."

Maybe I'm giving the senator more than his due, but that moment to me had some transcendental value which rose above the conflict and spoke from the soul of one man to the soul of another man, saying, "Life doesn't stop with the click of a camera shutter upon one awful second in existence, isolating it from all other seconds and minutes and hours. The camera runs on, connecting moments of anguish and despair with moments of joy and grace. Let the whole film tell the story, not one snapshot."

Some may say that Joe Biden was on the wrong side to offer such words. But for one shining moment, and for some reason perhaps unknown to him, Biden reached above the nauseous fog and clatter of conflicting wills, and found a side that had nothing to do with politics, but everything to do with the human soul.

Greenberg and others who see the senator patronizingly comparing his own hurt finger to the arm amputation of another man, miss something very important in the picture.

Biden wasn't cavalierly comparing his personal embarrassment over plagiarism with Thomas' anguish over what appeared to be the destruction of his life, although Biden may have included that in his thinking.

There had been other agonizing hours in Biden's experience when life seemed to have come to a heart-breaking halt, and from those unforgettable hours he addressed the agony in the soul of another man — not to vainly compare suffering with suffering, but to declare that life goes on beyond all suffering and loss.

Of course, there was the plagiarism and the hurt that went with it. But there was more. There was that awful day when the senator learned of the death of his wife and little girl. And there was more. There was the brain aneurism right in the midst of a presidential campaign which forced him to give up all he had hoped and worked for.

But as Biden reminded Thomas, life didn't stop with those moments of anguish; it went on. The camera was still rolling, and if he would let it, it would continue to roll for Clarence Thomas.

53. Who Are These Muslims Anyway?

What's wrong with Muslims? And why don't they like us? We share with them similar rich traditions. Abraham, Moses, Jesus — names both they and we know.

They are followers of the religion of Islam, one of the world's great religions. Bernard Lewis, a non-Muslim historian of Islam, writing in the September 1990 issue of *The Atlantic* magazine, speaks of the religion in almost glowing terms.

It "has brought comfort and peace of mind to countless millions of men and women. It has given dignity to drab and impoverished lives . . . It inspired a great civilization . . ."

But Islam — like some other religions, including Christianity, has known periods when it has inflamed some of its followers with the fires of hatred and violence.

It is the misfortune of our age that parts of the Muslim world are experiencing such a time, and much of the hatred generated is directed toward us Americans.

In the eyes of these Muslims, certainly not a majority, we of the West are cast in the role of "enemies of God."

While Islam is, like Christianity and Judaism, monotheistic, believing in one God, it has in the past come under the influence of Zoroastrianism, the religion of ancient Iran, which is dualistic.

Wherever its influence has reached — and it has been felt by Christianity and Judaism — the devil is a power equal in power to God. So this leaves God needing "believing" mortals to help Him in the eternal conflict.

In Islam the struggle between good and evil very early assumed political and military significance. Muhammad, its founder, in addition to being a teacher and a prophet, was a head of state and a soldier. So, the conflict as he viewed it, involved a state and its military forces.

From this view, it's an easy step to the conclusion that those who do battle for Islam in holy war "in the path of God" are fighting for God against God's enemies.

The army of Islam is the army of God; hence the enemies of Islam are fighting against God. God is the Commander In Chief of the armed forces.

According to the classical view of Islam, to which increasing numbers of Muslims are beginning to return, the whole world is divided into two camps: The House of Islam and the House of Unbelief.

But the greater part of the world is outside the House of Islam, and — even within Muslim lands — Islamic radicals see the faith being undermined and the law of Islam rejected by those who have fallen under western influence. So the object of attack in holy war is the infidel at home, and then the infidel abroad.

This may be where Saddam Hussein of Iraq makes his entrance. He has tried, and still is trying — and will no doubt keep on trying — to fan the sparks of conflict in the Middle East into a full-blown holy war of all Muslims against the United States. He hasn't succeeded yet, and may never.

For one big reason: Saddam Hussein himself is viewed by much of the Muslim world as one who has positioned himself on "the other side." He is viewed by devout Muslims as a man who scorns the best elements of Islam, yet exploits them for his own selfish purposes.

Saudi soldiers on the front lines with American GIs, who were interviewed while listening to Islamic prayer ballads on radio, confessed that their main objection to Saddam Hussein is not his grab for land and oil, but his secular ideology.

It's the Salman Rushdie situation all over again, in a sense. It would have been much less offensive to Iatola Koumeni if Rushdie, the author of *Satanic Verses*, which plays around with the Islamic faith, had never professed the Muslim faith.

But for him, one of their own, to deal with their sacred concepts with ridicule, cast him in a role worse than infidel —who for his own soul's sake deserves death, that in the afterlife he might be chastised.

These Muslims. We have met them in awesome military confrontation in Iraq. We meet them over oil. We meet them over points that divide us. And whether we like it or not, we'll be meeting them again and again in a shrinking, centripetal world, where all humanity is being thrown together.

Has the time come when we need to meet them on grounds of understanding? Moses is theirs and ours. Abraham is theirs and ours. And, in a sense, Jesus is theirs and ours.

54. Finding a Singular Faith in a Pluralistic Society

I've just been savoring some of the stately cadences of the *Koran*, the holy book of the Muslim religion. Excerpts of the sacred text were shared with me by a Muslim physician, a cardiologist, who once stood between me and death.

We've had brief dialogues on the subject of religion between cardiogram wiggles and stethoscope soundings of my dorsal and ventral areas.

Making due allowances for the intense gratitude which one feels toward a man who has saved one's life, there is a large admiration in me for this doctor as a human being. From some source, he has learned the ways of man's humanity to man. The law of kindness dwells in his heart, and the tender art of compassion is no stranger to him.

So when he handed me the holy words of the book which he has been taught to cherish and obey, I wanted to read them, remembering a quote from my own sacred book: "By their fruits ye shall know them."

If I had ever read these words of the *Koran*, I had forgotten their grandeur. As I read them, I was moved:

> "It is not righteousness
> That ye turn your faces
> Towards the East or West;
> But it is righteousness
> To believe in Allah . . .
> To spend of your substance,
> Out of love for Him,
> For your kin,
> For orphans,
> For the needy,
> For the wayfarer,
> For those who ask,
> And for the ransom of slaves;
> To be steadfast in prayer,
> And practice regular charity . . ."
> (*Koran*, Section 22, verses 177 through 180)

We are all living in a shrinking world, where people of diverse religions and cultures are drawn together — sometimes by war — as in the Gulf; sometimes in business; sometimes in love and marriage as in the house where my wife and I live, once owned by a Turkish Muslim and his Christian wife.

Insensitivity to differences in religions and the likenesses within the differences could be one of the flash points in a highly-combustible mixture, while sensitivity and mutual respect could prove to be a strong force to bind diverse cultures together.

So, there are the Muslims in the United States — three to five million of them. We'll be meeting them. Some of them will stand as a wall between us and death in operating rooms. Some will be neighbors. Some will be students. Some business men and women.

Like most of us, they believe in God. Their religious heritage is ours. Abraham, Moses, and Jesus are theirs.

Hear this:

> "O Mary! Allah gives thee
> Glad tidings of a Word
> From Him: his name
> Will be Christ Jesus,
> The son of Mary, held in honour
> In this world and the Hereafter."
>
> (*Koran*, Section 5, verse 45)

The United States is no longer the melting pot where all differences are obliterated in a grand amalgam. Instead it is becoming increasingly a place where diverse cultures and religions come face to face. Jew, Christian, Buddhist, Hindu, Muslim are evermore what they are without apology or concealment. We no longer — if we ever did — dwell in a white-Anglo Saxon-Protestant country.

Instead it's a white-black-red-yellow-Christian-Jew-Muslim-Buddhist country, where all people think of God in their own ways.

In such a pluralistic culture, awareness and respect for differences are important. Both insensitivity and hypersensitivity are hostile to peace and the human quest for God.

You'd think that by the time a man became Archbishop of Canterbury he would have achieved an unquestioning faith in God, wouldn't you?

Not so, says George Carey, Canterbury's archbishop, in an interview with David Aikman, reporting in September 2, 1991 *Time* magazine.

Aikman: "You once said you've never found it easy to believe in God. Why not?"

Carey: "I can identify with many people struggling with notions of faith. When you look at a world such as this and see, for example, the Holocaust when six million Jews perished and probably at least that number again of Christians and others who died. Now, they must have said their prayers, and yet God didn't deliver them. There are no glib answers to that sort of thing."

This is the thinking of an honest man of honest faith — not easy faith, mind you, but faith which has stood in the ring with hard-punching reality, has hit the mat more than once, but struggled up to fight some more.

A less honest man of such lofty ecclesiastical prominence could have been sorely tempted to disclaim any shadow of doubt, and might have bridled at the merest hint that his spiritual compass was the slightest degree off perfect reckoning.

This kind of honest confession lifts a burden from the souls of many of Carey's fellow mortals who struggle to sustain a faith in God in a world where faith is not always easy, and, for some, seems impossible.

Many people, in Carey's England and around the world, want to believe in God, but bitter experiences savage their souls and make them question what they so desperately want to believe.

And because they want a pure, unquestioning faith, they feel, as they have been taught since childhood, that to question or doubt is sin.

This adds one more burden to already burdened minds and sends them down shadowy paths of confusion, self-reproach, depression, even self-destruction.

Who needs a religion that beats on a man when he's already down and crying for help to make some sense out of his life in hard times and hard places?

No doubt Archbishop Carey would say that any believing person owes it to himself to make an appraisal of his faith —what he believes and why.

What do I expect of God? That he will do for me what I'm well able to do for myself? Come down and stir my coffee for me?

Do I expect that God will keep me from hurting myself if I defy gravity and make a headlong plunge from a window high up in the Empire State Building?

Do I expect, because I go to church and say my prayers and pay my tithe, that God will not let anything bad happen to me?

Ask Dave Dravecky, the young San Francisco Giants pitcher who, after weeks of prayer and exercise, regained the use of his pitching arm from a cancer operation, only to lose it in another operation when the cancer recurred.

Dravecky, who is still going on in his faith in God despite all that has happened, would likely say, with that strange, wonderful, never-give-up light in his eyes, "God lets some pretty awful things happen to us, but I still believe, because faith is what gives life meaning. It gave meaning to my life when I had two arms; it gives meaning now that I have only one."

That's not an easy faith, it's the faith of a fighter who refuses to let himself be cast in the role of victim.

For such men as Archbishop Carey and Dave Dravecky, faith is not easy because the facts of life are not easy, and both men are realists.

But their realism is bigger than the facts; it includes more. For them the God of their faith deals with vaster issues even than life and death. While, for many people, these are the boundaries of reality, for people who earn their faith the hard way, life and death with suffering and loss are boundaries which disappear in the boundless seas of God.

They are like those people of the early post-Columbian world who deleted the negative from their coins, which once read "Ne plus ultra" (No more beyond) and turned the words into a positive statement, "Plus ultra" (More beyond!).

56. Fall From Pride Is a Step Upward

It was a sadder but hopefully wiser Mayor Marion Barry of Washington, DC who stood, contrite and humble before the congregation of St. Timothy's Episcopal Church in the nation's capital and confessed: "This time I have come to face my deepest human failures. I've had to realize that God made Marion Barry the same as he made other people, a flesh and blood creation."

Sadder and wiser. Wiser in the sense of more realistic, closer to his own vulnerable human nature. Farther from the illusion that moved him to tell *The Los Angeles Times* two weeks earlier, "I'm invincible."

The man, whose rise was like a rocket blasting off from Cape Canaveral and whose administrative successes had grooved him into smooth orbit, had suddenly fallen from the sky.

Standing beside her husband at the podium of the church, Effi Barry told him, so that all could hear, "For you to admit to the world that you have a problem, that you need to deal with that problem . . . is truly a burden that has been lifted from our souls."

The mayor's subdued reply was: "I am going to find a way to begin to heal my mind, body, and soul."

There's a sense in which it was appropriate that this all took place within a Christian church where human beings are wont to acknowledge their limitations and sins and their dependence upon a power greater than themselves, where the words of Paul, the Christian apostle, are often heard: "Let no man that is among you think of himself more highly than he ought to think, but soberly, according as God has dealt to every man the measure of faith."

Appropriate, yes, but unusual, since some Christian churches have become identified with position and prestige. The tall steeple, magnificent architecture, colorful vestments, high pulpit, ornate altar — all of these have become symbols of congregational pride.

"The best people go here," is a line often heard in reference to a particular church building. "Best" meaning, of course, the most influential, wealthiest, best positioned.

Even ministers fall for this prideful line and immerse

themselves in the hubris of their congregations. The Christian Church which should help human beings humble themselves before God and man is often a bulwark of pride.

St. Timothy's pastor was no doubt glad to have the mayor in his congregation on Sunday mornings in the halcyon days of Barry's administration. And fellow parishioners no doubt took pride in the fact that they were members of "the mayor's church."

Now, with the penitent mayor's words still in their ears, and news of his fall in the newspaper headlines, St. Timothy's and all other churches have the opportunity to embrace their true ministry — helping men and women to join the mayor in humble confession of our human vulnerability.

There's little doubt that crack cocaine and alcohol contributed to Mayor Barry's "invincible" image of himself. But the church, which took pride in his pride and ensconced itself in his prestige, contributed also.

The way that Barry will find "to heal my mind, body, and soul" will be the way that the Christian Church, when it has been true to its Lord, has preached and taught and lived its gospel.

The healing will be more than a break with drugs and alcohol — they're symptoms of a deeper human illness. In St. Timothy's as in most Christian churches, there is a cross somewhere near the altar. It is the symbol of denial of the kind of human pride that precedes a fall.

The words which go with the symbol are a formula for recovery from the kind of egotism which sets itself up as a little tin god. This was the real "set up" that put Barry down. The words: "If any man will come after me, let him deny himself (as some kind of god), take up his cross and follow me."

57.   Let Your Private Faith Go Public

When a New Yorker tells another New Yorker to go to hell —in a subway or on an elevator (going down, of course) or in a bar, it doesn't make headlines.

But when a New Yorker who is a bishop tells another New

Yorker who happens to be the governor of New York that, if he doesn't change his ways, he's taking "a very serious risk of going straight to hell," that hits the papers and magazines and talk shows; and satellites beam it around the world.

It was Bishop Austin Vaughan of New York talking about Governor Mario Cuomo of New York, and it was plain talk with some hell fire in it.

Cuomo, never short on words himself, fired back, "My position is very simple: I think I am the governor of all the people. It is not my place to try to convert all of them . . . and insist they believe the way I privately believe they should live."

This position is well-founded in American politics and rests on John Kennedy's statement before a group of Houston Protestant ministers in 1960: "I believe in an America where the separation of church and state is absolute — where no . . . prelate would tell the President . . . how to act."

As a candidate for the highest office in the land, JFK declared that he would decide issues "in accordance with what my conscience tells me to be the national interest, and without regard to outside religious pressures or dictates."

This all sounds fair enough and downright American, doesn't it? But as *Time* writer, John Elson, asks in a recent article, "Why should not the church play a role in forming and guiding the conscience of its adherents?"

So Bishop Vaughan might appropriately ask, "Mario (or whatever else he may be calling the governor by this time), do you think you can believe something as strongly as I think you do, and not have it make any difference in what you say or do beyond the safe and secure walls of the church?"

"But Bishop, as I say, I'm governor of all the people . . ."

"Yes, Governor, I heard you say that earlier, but Jesus Christ is the Lord of all who believe in him, and you do believe in him, don't you, Governor?"

"But I've been elected by the people to be Governor of New York . . ."

"True, but you have elected, of your own free will, to be a Christian within a church which declares itself to be against abortion — a position that you confess you yourself privately accept."

"But I've been elected . . ."

"Governor, it comes down to this, either give up your private faith or make it as public as your three-piece suits and your shoes and neckties and your after-shave lotion. If your faith is an embarrassment to you, Mario, perhaps you should give it up — if indeed you haven't done so already."

This might-have-been dialogue is not a single-issue one. It touches every area of life. It's not merely the question of separation of church and state; it's the question of separation of faith and life.

Human beings don't live their lives in the mellow glow of stained-glass windows. They live in the world. And the world has the right to expect to feel the impact of what they say they believe when they're in church.

There's been a debate in progress for centuries over this issue. It reaches back to the earliest Christian decades to a brief literary piece that bears the by-line of a writer by the name of James.

"What does it profit, my brethern," he writes, "if a man says he has faith but has not works . . . Faith by itself, if it has no works, is dead."

Carrying his point a step further, the writer says "even the devils believe," and he might have added, "But it doesn't make a devil of a difference to any of them."

People who count on a do-nothing faith to save them and save the world are like words written on water.

58. God in Williamsburg

Our decision to go down to Williamsburg for the Fourth of July was not the result of profound thought or patriotic fervor. It just happened, you might say. We wanted to get away for a few days following our wedding anniversary celebration. So we said, "Let's take a while off during the week following the week of our anniversary."

"Where shall we go?"

"How about Williamsburg?"

So we made our reservations at the Motor House Motel and immediately got swallowed up in the anniversary plans. Then one morning at breakfast came this:

"You know something?"

"What?" I asked.

"We'll be in Williamsburg over the Fourth of July!"

It was only then that the drums began to beat in our heads and fifes began to pipe, and yards of red white and blue bunting floated through our thoughts.

Williamsburg on the Fourth!

To be there at any time is to receive a new baptism in the spirit that made America; but to be there on America's national birthday and witness the review of the "colonial" troops and hear the cannon and muskets firing over the green and smell the powder smoke drifting in the summer breeze — well, that would be patriotic bliss.

Williamsburg, where Thomas Jefferson attended William and Mary College, and where Patrick Henry and Jefferson and other leaders of the Revolution worshipped in historic old Bruten Parish Church on the wide boulevard dotted with shops and inns.

It was here that men first talked about "Nature's God" by whom "all men were created equal." Here's where the mind of Jefferson ripened and was made ready to frame the daring words which later flowed from his pen onto America's greatest document, the Declaration of Independence.

Through the thinking born in Williamsburg, the world that was England was about to be turned upside down. The old world in which subjects petitioned kings was to be turned inside out on the spearhead of a great new idea which, in the mind of Jefferson, became a passionate belief.

That idea centered in the view that "Nature's God," not kings or governments, is the source of all human rights, and these rights to "Life, liberty, and the pursuit of happiness" are "unalienable," which meant to the colonists that they are structured into the very nature of the world as God created it. These God-given rights, Jefferson and his fellow colonists believed, are morally superior to the power of any government.

At the outset, the colonists had petitioned for their rights as Englishmen under English law. The Declaration of Independence took a bold step beyond this.

They took another daring step when they declared that kings and governments exist for the purpose of protecting these divine rights — not of kings but of ordinary men and women.

They kept going — giant step after giant step, leap after daring leap. Since governments exist for the purpose of protecting these "divine rights" of everyday people, any government which fails to protect them should likely be overthrown.

And the story is not over yet. The influence of Jefferson's pen is being felt in Poland and in the provinces of Soviet Russia, and in China where the words of the Declaration of Independence have echoed through Tianamin Square, and Patrick Henry's booming voice has been heard coming from the lips of Chinese students, "Give me liberty or give me death!"

Those men of Williamsburg were believers, and as Clare Boothe Luce once said, "For a people, as for a person, believing is all. All history bears witness that it is the believers who win the revolutions, found nations, conquer the oceans, tame the wilderness, raise up great cities and great institutions. The doubters, the cynics, the unbelievers — they can scarsely shake the pebbles from their shoes, much less move mountains."

59. God on TV?

It happened without a lot of fanfare. No waving of signs. No attention-grabbing slogans. Maybe you didn't even notice it — but God's back!

And of all the "unholy" places — TV. The much-maligned medium, notorious purveyor of glutted sex and mayhem, has fingered the pulse of the times and felt the throb of desire for God.

Prime-time networks are turning out scripts which make room for characters to be religious without embarrassment or apology.

There's ABC-TV's highly successful show "Thirtysomething." Michael, played by Ken Olin, is a young Jew who hasn't seen the inside of a synagogue much since his bar mitzvah. He's married to Hope, played by Mel Harris, who for obituary purposes and other terminal announcements, is a Christian.

In an episode highlighting the winter holidays, the two of them are debating whether they should introduce their little girl to the Christian yuletide tradition or to Hanukkah.

An easy out for them (and the writers) would have been to assume a jaunty sophisticated attitude and behave like neither of the religious traditions mattered, so "let's just forget the whole thing."

Instead, both of them discovered they had their own personal religious needs and honored each other's. The show closed with a poignant scene.

Michael, feeling the warm glow of reconciliation with his own religious past, comes home carrying a Christmas tree to help Hope in introducing their daughter to Christmas. Struggling with the tree, he runs into Hope, lighting the first candle in a menorah to help him share the Feast of Lights with their little girl.

There's another episode where baby-boomer Michael, having impressions of the clergy as *old* and *fuddy-duddy*, is shocked out of his baby-boomer mind when he drops into a synagogue for the first time in years. Instead of an old man, white of mane and beard, moving in the glow of the eternal flame, there is a hip young rabbi, still in his thirties. Taken aback, but grateful, he slips into Sabbath worship, and life seems good again.

By the good graces of Bill Moyers, Baptist minister turned general commentator on many subjects including religion, God has made it on PBS.

Moyers interviews with Joseph Campbell, discussing Campbell's book, *The Power of Myth,* in which the religious values of diverse cultures are investigated. These interviews won a large audience and brought an overwhelming response. His "God and Politics" was similarly successful.

Another documentary, "The Supreme Court's Holy Battles," examined the heated controversy over separation of church and state. It brought out some thought-provoking facts about our American political and religious history, revealing close intimate ties between religious faith and the foundations of democracy.

Comedy is another TV genre which has received baptism as a vehicle to convey religious values in a secular world. For starts, there was NBC-TV's show "Amen." In a contemporary black Protestant congregation some funny things happen, and sinners reach out to touch the trailing garments of divine grace as they muddle through their nights and days.

"Amen" opened the way for another religious comedy, "Bless Me, Father." This show carousels around a Roman Catholic priest, played by Arthur Lowe. After a successful run in England, it has been seen on a number of PBS affiliates.

Still another one, "Have Faith" (ABC-TV) features a team of clerics in humorous situations as they minister to their flocks. Despite their occasional ineptness and mistakes, these funny men of the cloth are clearly seen as instruments of God's grace.

So, it you twirl your TV dial or run the cycle of your remote, you will no doubt find, at some point between heavy gunfire and heavy breathing, a gentle reminder that the human soul still longs for God.

60.   I Didn't Know God Could Be So Physical

Thumping on my chest. A dim remote awareness. Not the slightest glimmering of question why it should be happening or what it meant.

Then a shock, and with the shock a flash of light.

I felt something strike my head, and asked, "What's that?"

A feminine voice apologized.

Another voice said, "He's talking!"

I opened my eyes and looked around. I was surrounded by a huddle of nurses, clinicians, and doctors.

"Looks like we're having a party here," I said.

"We are, and we're glad you decided to join us," someone

said.

Was it death? Could death be like this? So gentle, so like falling asleep at the end of a weary day?

I remember feeling drowsy, lying on the hospital bed in ICU at Nanticoke Memorial Hospital in Seaford, Delaware. Then came that sleep, gentler than sleep.

Return to life. Was this the meaning of the violent beating on my chest? Then the shock like a bolt of lightning. Was this what it took to wake me from that deep, gentle, dreamless sleep?

Yes to all the above. So I've learned since. The marvelous little fist-size pump just below my breast bone, after beating more than two and a half billion times, had stopped pumping. No action. Blood pumped at the rate of five quarts a minute to every cell of the body was lying motionless in veins and arteries, incapable of moving.

That's when Code 99 sounded over the speaker system, and nurses, lab personnel, and doctors came running to do what they could do. And what they could do — with muscle power and the power of 400 joules of electricity flowing through two "paddles" on my chest, was enough to get my heart jump-started and beating again.

And now I have time to think and try to get it all together. I realize this was one of those near-death experiences which Elizabeth Kubler Ross has written about so convincingly.

But, no, I didn't have any out-of-body flights. I never looked down on my body from some remote corner of the ceiling in ICU.

I don't recall any dark tunnel passage. I did see a brilliant flash of light at the moment of the electric shock. I didn't see any dear, departed loved ones waiting for me. (Maybe it all happened too suddenly for anybody to get the reception committee together.)

Or it may have been I wasn't far enough gone for these things. And I completely missed the feeling of joy in forever learning. Maybe next time.

In Christiana Hospital in Wilmington, Delaware, where I was transferred to receive heart catheterization, among the questions asked was this one: Will this episode of illness make any difference in your religious life? (A question no doubt made part of the questionnaire by the Pastoral Ministries Department.)

When the nurse asked the question, I thought a moment

then said "No."

No meant that I thought there would be no negative effects upon my spiritual life. What I overlooked was the powerful, positive effect of all this. That effect has been building through the hours and days since.

Part of it is a warm feeling that my life is not a solitary enterprise, a solo flight. There are other hands than mine helping me. Other wills than mine, urging, "Live . . . Live!"

And though I didn't see dear familiar faces from "the other side" waiting for me a' la Kubler Ross, I have seen dear familiar faces waiting for me on this side: wife, sons, daughters-in-love, grandsons, and a little granddaughter.

And though I did not feel the benign presence in that deeper-than-deep sleep, I have felt a dear benign presence welcoming me back into life, assuring me that I am never alone.

Not some vague, impersonal, mystical presence, but something very personal, very real, and infinitely close to me. One who knows my name even without reading it on the little wrist bands. (I had two of them — one for each hospital.)

A power and presence that works in marvelous ways to restore me to health through legions of white blood cells called *phagocytes,* clearing out the debris of the blood clot that blocked one of the coronary arteries and caused the heart attack.

I'm sure the medical professionals who helped me so much won't be offended if I call these little guys "God's angels," working for me night and day without change of shifts or time off.

They're in there now, under a command higher than mine, clearing the vital channels, making way for a more adequate blood supply to that blessed little pump that faltered once and stopped, but with help got started again.

Had I forgotten? Or did I ever really know that God could be so physical, and so physically involved?

Whatever I have ever believed has taken a quantum leap. Faith has crossed over a border, and lives and breathes with fact.

And now — to live again.

61. There's Nothing Like a Brush With Mortality to Get Attention

There's nothing like a chilling hint of mortality to open the choked channels between a human being and others. Include in *others* the "Ultimate Other" whom we call God.

It happened to George Bush, President of the United States, recently when he was jogging at Camp David as usual and something unusual happened. The steady rhythm of the heart lost its vital timing like a car's cylinders misfiring. There followed a shortness of breath, a pounding in the chest, a frightening weakness.

There had been an earlier close encounter with death when at age 20 Bush was fished out of the Pacific after bailing out of his burning plane and bobbing like a cork for several hours before the U.S.S. Finback picked him up. Bush claimed later that after he was safely aboard the submarine he took time "to talk to God." But life went on and the experience was pushed aside to make way for "more important" things.

However, with that near stalling of his engine at the age of 66, echoes of the earlier experience returned. There are hints in what he has said since then that the busy life of the President has made way for some serious reflections upon mortality.

There has been a cracking of what has been called Bush's "patrician reserve," and a new, more relaxed man stands and strides and talks before the world, a man more in touch with his own faith and feelings.

Unashamed and only superficially apologetic for misty eyes and a quaver in his voice, he spoke about prayer and God in a 17-minute address to the members of the Southern Baptist Convention in Atlanta, Georgia. The President confessed openly to tears as he prayed for the American troops on the day that Operation Desert Storm began. Bush said, "Now I no longer worry about how I look to others. With prayer, what matters is how it seems to God."

Is this just one of those "new images," a political ploy to make the President seem more a man of the people — a good image for the coming presidential campaign?

Critical observers, as well as close friends, claim that it's not a radical change in the man himself. They think it's the emergence of a side of him held back for years and now released by his recent close brush with death.

It may have something to do with Lee Atwater, Bush's old friend, former campaign manager, and Republican Party head.

Atwater at the early age of 39 had his own encounter with mortality when he learned that he had a brain tumor which was inoperable.

The news was devastating to Atwater, his family and friends, but he determined to fight the cancer as he had fought many a political foe — by discovering its weak point and working on it. However, he could find no weak point in the enemy; it was in himself.

That's when he began to become a different man. "I was never a religious man," says Atwater in the February 1991 issue of *Life*. "If you asked me, I would have said I was a Christian, but I didn't go to church and can't pretend that I relied on my faith for much of anything."

"Confronted by the prospect of my own end, I reevaluated things. 'Know yourself,' wrote Plato. Now I realized that knowing yourself includes knowing your relationship with your maker."

So began Atwater's serious spiritual quest. He talked with everyone who would talk with him about God, including Chuck Colson; Pat Robertson; the Bushes, who had lost a daughter to leukemia; and Secretary Baker, who had lost a wife to cancer. He even watched children's religious cartoons with his children. For the first time in his life he read the Bible.

But, says Atwater, as long as he treated his search for faith as an intellectual exercise, little happened. Then someone told him that faith is not intellectual; it's a kind of leap, letting go to God.

"I sensed a new spiritual presence in my life — something that arrived without my having to call it . . . I felt at peace."

He found himself reaching out to other patients. When a group of kids visited a friend who had sustained a gunshot wound, Atwater talked with them about what is important in life.

A new, caring man emerged in the hospital bed where Atwater lay, a man who apologized for his mistreatment of others — including Michael Dukakis, about whom he had said he'd strip his bark off.

The awareness of mortality breathing its cold breath close to life's warm pulse truly opens up the clogged channels between man and man, man and God, and man and his own true self.

62.   Back to Kindergarten for Washington Big Boys

The big boys in Washington are sitting down like little boys to learn what many of them learned as little boys but forgot when they became big boys.

Yep — they're back "in school," re-learning what they learned as kids — what's right and what's wrong.

Robert Fulghum, author of the popular book, *All I Really Need To Know I Learned In Kindergarten,* admits that it wasn't in the higher grades of his educational career that he learned how to behave as a decent human being; it was in the sandpile at Sunday School.

So, many of the big boys from Capitol Hill to the Pentagon are back in morality's kindergarten, re-learning the difference between good and bad.

Dan Fesperman, who writes for *The Baltimore Sun* and knows a whole lot more than I know about Washington, says there's a big demand for the services of a growing number of businesses which specialize in teaching honesty and good behavior under the name of ethics.

Ethics is "the science of moral values and duties, the study of … human character, actions, and ends," according to Webster.

Sounds impressively sophisticated, doesn't it? But when you make your way through the welter of words, what it's all about is plain, everyday right and wrong, and whether a person's behavior falls on the shady side of the line or the sunny side.

And the big boys who are nervous over questions about their behavior are going to pay big money (or taxpayers will have to pay the bill for them) to go back to kindergarten under the tutelage of the great Judeo-Christian ethic which has helped mightily to keep the human race straight through the millenia.

They won't have to fork out much at first. For $150, a video package can be purchased to re-teach the ethically wayward how to get back on track.

Even defense contractors who, without blinking a jaundiced eye, asked for — and got — $6,000 apiece for monkey wrenches, can begin their moral reform while waiting nervously for the auditor's knock on the office door.

The bigger money hits them later — when they get really serious about coming clean, or want to create the impression that they're on the level.

One of the experts in straightening out crooked characters is Michael Josephson, who heads an ethics-tutoring company based in California.

He charges $5,000 to $15,000 for an ethics workshop. He reports that there are so many businesses and government agencies wanting to clean up their acts that he had to turn down more requests for services last year than he accepted.

Apparently the desperate rush to the altar for conversion started with a highly publicized series of unethical shenanigans in government and government-related business and industry.

There were those insider-trading scandals that rocked Wall Street. A movie based on the scandals got a lot of people thinking, especially when the film character, Gordon Gecko, the billionaire adventurer, brazenly affirmed his creed, "Greed is good."

And when Beech Nut was caught with its water faucets running, selling sugar water as nutritious apple juice for little babies, a lot of people got mad.

Then there were the cost overruns and rip-offs, featuring characters without character monkeying around with those $6,000 monkey wrenches to help keep good old Uncle Sam and his nephews and nieces safe from their enemies.

On top of all this, came the fall of smiling Jim Wright, Speaker of the House of Representatives, who — apparently —improved his net worth appreciably through a shady publishing deal.

So, it's back to kindergarten and Sunday School and

synagogue school, boys. Back to "Thou shalt have no other gods before me" (including the shiny little god called money). Also, "Thou shall not covet . . ." And, "Thou shalt not steal." Plus, "Thou shalt not bear false witness . . ."

63.   Don't Forget the Baby!

Bite your tongue on the "B word." If you feel you must say it, speak softly so as not to offend anyone. Better still, stick with the cool, clinical, antiseptic terms, words that do not come thundering into the station with heavy emotional freight.

When a speaker ventured recently to utter the tabooed word, there was a quick disapproving response from one person in the audience.

The occasion was a meeting of the National Conference of Catholic Bishops in Baltimore, Maryland. The topic on the agenda was the hot one — abortion.

Archbishop John May, who had the floor, simply said, "Don't forget the baby. That's all the Catholic Church is saying to America."

No sooner had the "B word" — baby — been spoken than Frances Kissling, representing Catholics for a Free Choice, called the comment "cruel and unusual punishment for the Catholic and non-Catholic women who decide to have abortions."

Since I wasn't present at the conference, and so missed any inflections, gestures, or facial expressions at the podium which may have seemed sinister or threatening, I have only the plain simple words to go on: "Don't forget the baby."

This seems to suggest that in the furor kindled by the highly-charged polarity of pro-choice and pro-life, it's possible for the word-and-idea people to forget that somewhere in the tangled threads of argument and counterargument, there lies between "to be or not to be," an innocent and helpless baby.

If it is "cruel and unusual punishment" to link the tender word *baby* with the harsh, wrenching word "abortion," it's the cruelty of truth.

The alternative is to pretend there is no baby, never was a baby, and never could have been a baby. Anaesthetize the conscience with a lie, and the whole thing can be managed without spiritual pain. A piece of cake!

Let Raquel Welch claim liberation from any trace of guilt over an abortion, as she did on the Larry King Show. Her smiling, chirpy response to a probing question about her feelings was blithely frightening, like something heard in an audience in revolutionary Paris around the guillotine.

Can we be convinced that a human life which has begun to develop — whatever the stage of development — is not a human life, but a mass of impersonal, undifferentiated tissue? If so, we are dangerously close to the "big lie," which could be turned against us all — if or when our human existence might become inconvenient or uncomfortable to somebody.

We human beings have a frightening way of reducing to the "thing" level any individual or group which we don't want to be bothered with as human beings.

If we want to exploit *them* without suffering the pain of violated Christian consciences, we declare they are less than human, as Christian gentlemen did with black slaves.

If we want to exterminate them, we consider them animals for the slaughter, as we do with "the enemy" in warfare, and as the Nazis did with the Jews as they herded them into the gas chambers.

Only for people dedicated to this kind of reductionist thinking is the word "baby" offensive when raised as part of the great abortion battle.

They'll talk glibly about "the fetus" and "a woman's right to her own body," but don't offend them by telling them simply, "Don't forget the baby."

I'm not for laying guilt on anyone. I've spent many hours helping to relieve men and women of their guilt by obliging them to face the truth of their behavior, not by taking refuge in a lie.

This is the honest way to deal with life. Not to devalue it so that its hurts no longer hurt, but to cherish and respect it in all its forms and grieve when it is hurt.

"Don't forget the baby!"

64.   Bring Downstairs Upstairs

"Let me play devil's advocate," I said in a phone interview with Gerry Wagner in Harrisburg, Pennsylvania, who was representing Bishop Felton May, whom I couldn't reach.

"What on earth can the church do to even make a dent in the armor plate of the drug tank rumbling through the nation's capital?"

I wanted to hear what kind of approach Bishop May had in mind as the United Methodist Church's man to spearhead the denomination's anti-drug attack in Washington, D.C.

I heard words like "evangelistic," "moral-spiritual dimension," "multi-pronged approach," "the best values," "create a climate," and "guerilla warfare" (which I naturally interpreted in the spiritual sense).

What I hoped to hear — and may hear as time goes on — is that the twelve Washington churches selected to participate in the opening phase of the attack would be carefully readied to become spiritual "combat units."

This brings me to say that, if the church is to be effective in licking the nation's drug problem, it should take a good look at what's happening in its own basement.

Down there, among the dusty props of last year's Christmas pageant: angel wings, tinsel haloes, wise men's crowns, and shepherds' staffs, there's a group of people who meet quietly week after week.

These people know more about the drug problem and care more about it than George Bush or Bill Bennett, or anybody else whose name appeared in headlines as generals in the great drug war.

They not only know more about it, they're doing more about it — fighting where the battle is the hottest, in their own personal lives.

If you think I'm talking about AA, you're right. Throughout the nation, groups of men and women meet regularly — often in church basements, not merely to talk about the problem but to attack it head on. And they win and keep on winning.

Some of them may venture up into the church sanctuary occasionally, but it's not "upstairs" that they find strength to fight and keep on fighting. It's "downstairs" where AA meets.

Not that they don't appreciate stained-glass windows, choirs, organ music, ritual prayers, and religious pageantry. It's just that all this doesn't seem to meet them where they live.

If the church is to be more than a plaintive squeak amid the thunder claps of the great drug storm, it needs to bring "upstairs" and "downstairs" together.

Go down and tell those people meeting in church basements, "Come on up!" Or let them extend the invitation, "Come on down!"

Then let clergymen and board members, and all the worshipful gathering sit down and hear what these people have to say about addiction and how they're overcoming it in their own lives.

Alcoholics Anonymous and other Twelve-Step support groups learned what they know from the church. The Oxford Movement, a small-group discipline active in the 1920s and 30s, from which AA learned its successful strategy for dealing with addiction, had its roots deep in the life of the Christian Church. It was there that honest self-examination, acknowledgement of character defects, restitution for harm done to others, and commitment of one's will to the will of God had their beginnings.

To be effective in today's drug world, the church needs to rediscover its own dynamic for changing human lives. In earlier times the United Methodist Church and its antecedents encouraged small-group meetings on a weekly basis. They were called "class meetings." Individuals used to ask one another, as naturally as they passed the time of day, "How is it with your soul?" They expected and received an answer, while giving and receiving strong support.

            # Faith Tried by Fire

The year 1991 witnessed the liberation of hostages from Beirut, Lebanon, where some prisoners had been held for more than five years.

Thus ended a period which revealed the nastiest features of man's inhumanity to man. But it also revealed something else: The capacity of the human spirit to endure, survive, even overcome, when all visible supports have been removed.

What sustains a human being who is forced to live day by day, often in solitary confinement, frequently blindfolded, sometimes chained, treated like an animal, receiving food under a cell door? What inner resources come to one's rescue to resist despair and self-loathing?

Take the case of Terry Anderson. For six years he was confined to a dark cell, often alone and chained, brutalized by his captors, tortured physically and mentally.

Following his release, Anderson was asked by reporters in Damascus how he managed during those six harrowing years.

"You wake up every day, summon up the energy from somewhere and you get through the day, day after day after day," he said.

He confessed there were quite a few times when, worn down with suffering and near despair, he felt like giving up. But he held on.

The first book he was permitted to have in his cell was a Bible. He read it through, feeding his soul on the great narratives, poetry, letters, and wisdom literature.

In the mighty rhythms he found strength: The days and nights of Genesis slipped into the weary repetition of his own nights and days, adding a touch of meaning. The forgotten Edens . . . Red Seas to cross into liberation . . . a young man sold into slavery, a stranger in a strange land . . . men singing in jail at midnight . . . stories of survivors who through faith became "more than conquerors."

Gradually, as opportunity came, and he dialogued with fellow hostages, Anderson felt the warm tide of his youthful Catholic faith returning.

When asked what kept him going during those nights and

days, Anderson mentions his faith and personal stubbornness. To these he adds his contacts with other hostages, with whom he was thrown from time to time.

This was the winning combination for Anderson. Each part of the triad fed the other two. Faith fed his natural, dogged stubbornness and determination not to be overwhelmed, and stubbornness fed companionship as Anderson determined to keep his sanity by sharing ideas with others. And sharing in dialogues of honest confession became the spring through which his faith was renewed.

From another hostage named Terry — Terry Waite, held in Beirut for nearly five years, the story is similar. As the fifty-two-year-old Anglican breathed his earliest breaths of freedom, his relatives and colleagues were telling reporters that he is "a man of very deep Christian faith." Church bells pealed over England when Waite and Thomas Sutherland, the American hostage, had been freed.

Charles Sesaretti, an Episcopal Church official and close friend of Waite, told Religious News Service that Waite weathered the storm well, and will emerge from the experience with important theological insights about suffering. "We will be quite struck by the ways he has . . . grown during this time," he said.

Far from being lost years, the years of imprisonment may well turn out to be among the most productive years in the lives of the hostages, now liberated, as they reveal more of the strengths of the human spirit, which surfaced and surrounded them in their deepest agony and darkest hours. A time of growth, a time of insight through suffering. As the bells in England's church towers were ringing toward year's end of 1991, they were celebrating the victory of the human spirit and its triumph over life's most brutalizing experiences.

When the Redskins and the Bills mixed it up on the artificial turf of the Metrodome on Super Bowl Sunday, they didn't look exactly like they had just come from a prayer meeting.

The big guys didn't seem to fit the picture of hymn singers or Bible toters. Football and religion are worlds apart — or so it seemed to thousands of spectators crowding the stands.

But don't bet your upper dentures on it! Why? Because there's a strong movement going the other way — from those gladiators themselves.

Are you ready for this? Before and after the big game, according to an article in the *National and International Religion Report* of January 27, 1992, members of the Buffalo Bills and Washington Redskins prayed together.

If that rocks you, get this: Along with popcorn, hot dogs, drinks, and game notes making their way through the stands, there were thousands of printed pieces naming nineteen Redskins who pray regularly and confess the lordship of Jesus Christ in their lives.

Names? Here are some of them: Earnest Byner, Ricky Ervins, Charles Mann, Art Monk, Darrell Green, and Ricky Sanders. Each one of these man had signed a release for the use of his name in the folder.

Some of the Redskin fans knew, but a lot didn't know — or had forgotten — that the Washington team holds chapel service at home and away games, led by Lee Corder of Harrisonburg, Virginia, serving his fourth year as Redskins volunteer chaplain.

At home games, forty to eighty members of the team, along with family members, attend Saturday evening chapel. On the road, fifteen to twenty players attend.

Wednesday evenings see members of the team and their wives engaging in home Bible studies, according to Corder. Some of them are active in churches of the Washington area, and head community programs for youth. "These guys have a platform to make a difference with kids, especially those in the cities, and I've seen some have a wonderful impact," Corder says.

Meanwhile, in the Bills' camp, a group of players meets every Monday morning during the playing season with Fred Raines, who has been the team's chaplain for eight years. Mark Kelso, Frank Fiech, Howard Ballard, Pete Metzelaars, Dwight Drane, James Lofton, Carlton Bailey, and others are among them.

Now sit back, take a deep breath, and guess what they do. "They memorize Scripture, share testimonies, and learn how to witness without fear," Raines says. "Each has another guy on the team under his wing," Raines adds.

Kicker Scott Norwood, who shares a room with Kelso on the road, acknowledged to a reporter that he had recently accepted Christ.

Muscular Christianity stepped forward, flexed its muscles, and declared its faith in 1991. It was the year when the Chicago Bears and New York Giants joined in a prayer circle on the field following the playoff game in January. Spectators didn't know whether to cheer or cry or just sit on their hands.

That was the year, too, when Los Angeles Dodger Darryl Strawberry hit the front page of the *New York Times* in a story about religious conversion, and tithing of big salaries among professional athletes. Again, fans didn't know what to make of such behavior, but the guys did.

Then there was that time back in June when the Chicago Bulls prayed the Lord's Prayer after winning the NBA playoffs.

What's it all about? What's happening? One answer seems to be that these guys feel it's time to come out of the closet with the best that is in them, time to kick off the bushels hiding their candles, and let them shine.

With so many creeps coming out in the open with faces unashamed, they may feel it's time to open the closet door on their own sincere faith.

If evil can shame good people into closeting the best that is in them, while evil itself parades around shameless as an angel of light, there's something sadly wrong.

So here's a big cheer for the guys who are big enough, strong enough, sure enough of themselves and their relationship with God to kick the *shame* and step out where they can challenge the rest of us to do the same.

67. Outlaws in a Universe of Laws

"When was the last time you had a good conversation about sin?"

This question did not come from a preacher in some lofty pulpit on Sunday morning, with Bible, organ music, stained-glass windows, and clerical vestments asserting his right to ask such a question.

It wasn't even in a religious journal or the religion section of Saturday's newspaper — although that's getting close. Actually it was in the business section of the *New York Times* of January 8, 1992, at the bottom of a full-page ad.

The ad was a reprint of an editorial which first appeared in the *Wall Street Journal* of December 12, 1991, a 900-word piece under the heading "The Joy of What?"

The editorial, which evoked much favorable comment, condemns the moral license of the so-called sexual revolution, and deplores highly-publicized scandals featuring public figures.

Daniel Henninger, the writer of the *Wall Street Journal* editorial, says it's time to speak up on the subject, because "a lot of people are intimidated into keeping their mouths shut about the old-fashioned notion of sin."

Sin, says Henninger, "isn't something that many people, including most churches, have spent much time talking about or worrying about through the years of the (sexual) revolution."

Commenting on the big-banner headlines dedicated to the Earvin "Magic" Johnson story, he says, "With a few dissenting exceptions, 96 hours and 96 zillion column inches of sentiment washed over the falls about how all this proved the need for 'safe sex,' before someone finally said that Magic Johnson's sex life was simply wrong."

If Johnson had been as wrong on the basketball court, he would have been thrown out of the sport long ago. Are there rules for basketball and no rules for living? Are there penalties for fouls committed on the gleaming floor and none for fouls committed in the game of life?

Translated into basketball terms, sin would be acting like there were no rules, no referee — nothing to keep the game from becoming a free-for-all, with spectators hopping down from the stands, grabbing the ball, and doing whatever they wanted to do.

Sin, the word which the *Wall Street Journal* invoked with editor Henninger, rushes in where the timid angels of the churches fear to tread. Aided by its ancient roots and multiple, modern branches, sin continues, largely unabated.

Essentially it means behaving as though we were not responsible to anyone except ourselves, and had no rules except our own desires, ambitions, and satisfactions. In other words, "If it feels good, do it!"

We're in big trouble, and the reason is that *we're outlaws in a universe of laws.* We act like there is no law, no source of law, and no penalty — or, if there is, we choose to ignore them as in Kipling's "Road to Mandalay." "Where there ain't no Ten Commandments and the best is like the worst." So, we commit lawless exploitation of earth, skies, seas, fellow human beings, other life forms, and ourselves.

In the process, *we disturb finely-tuned balances of nature and human nature, and reap frightening consequences.* We're wrong, and not just economically, socially, and politically — on a scale where a little fixing of this and that will make things right. We're wrong down deep where the issues of life and death are drawn.

When we get on the wrong side of right things — of what some people call Nature, and others of us call God — we can expect to have our hands slapped and our knuckles rapped just to remind us that we're off limits.

So, if our knuckles are aching and the backs of our hands are smarting, we ought to sit up and pay attention. Whether we want to consider a depleting ozone shield above us or AIDS within us as the punishment of an offended God or a violated Nature, something's rapping our knuckles, and *we're smart if we pay attention and dumb if we don't.*

68.   The Blessed Disillusionment

This week, more Americans prayed than went to work, jogged, ran, used exercise machines, or engaged in sex. That's a lot of praying!

So reports the first issue of *Newsweek* for this new year of 1992. The report is based on studies by Andrew M. Greely, well-known priest, sociologist, and novelist, working at NORC, a research center.

The studies reveal that 78 percent of Americans pray at least once a week, and more than half — 57 percent — say they pray at least once a day. Now hear this: even atheists and agnostics admit that they pray daily — one in five of them.

Some of these prayers are *in extremis* — from people swirling around in the vortex of a personal or family crisis: sickness, marital problems, loss of job, etc. Among the eight and a half million Americans out of work, no doubt more prayers than usual are going up.

But these situations don't explain all of the prayers offered up by three quarters of the population of the United States. There seems to be a hunger and thirst in the American soul, which cars, houses, TVs and VCRs can't satisfy. It's a longing for God that, according to the studies, begins after the age of thirty — "when the illusion that we are masters of our own fate fades and adults develop a deeper need to call on the Master of the Universe." (*Newsweek,* January 6, 1992)

This means that true prayer begins at the point where a human being makes a realistic assessment of his position in the universe.

There are stages in human development when we think we're "It" — that we're independent, self-made, self-sustaining, even omnipotent and immortal. When a human being confers such power and glory upon himself, who needs God?

This creature immodesty is forgivable when one considers the fact that the intelligence and power which designed and created us did such exquisite work that the illusion of independence is possible.

Edison, in his design and creation of the incandescent light bulb, did such a good job that light can flood into a dark room by the flip of a switch without any thought about Edison. So, it's possible to live with a body so well made and finely tuned that an individual can live a lifetime without giving any thought to his/her Maker.

You might say that the very efficiency and modesty of God in not interjecting himself into his creation may permit us to ignore him.

It's only when a few chinks appear in our armor that we experience the blessed disillusionment which turns us at last toward God. When you can wake in the morning and see the world with 20-20 vision, when all the colors and shapes are bright and clear, it's easy, and even natural, to assume that it's *you* doing the seeing, without any assistance from beyond you.

But when your 20-20 begins to fade, you may give some thought to the marvelous design of cornea, lens, retina, and optic nerve which make it all possible.

Then, when you realize, as you must, that you are not the designer and maker of this superb optical equipment, you may turn to some point beyond you and say "Thank you!"

However, it's not merely awareness of our human vulnerability and dependence which turn men and women toward God. There's something deeper, something more like the soul reaching out for its greatest possible joy and fulfillment through communion with its Source.

"We are all making the search, whether we know it or not." So says Father Charles Gonzales, rector of the Jesuit community at Georgetown University in Washington, D.C.

Prayer, ultimately, is a love affair with God. All human beings need the touch of unconditional love upon their lives; and in a world where many *love*-relationships fail to yield such love, the human soul will seek and find it in the "love divine."

69.   Damned by Low Expectations

Was there ever a time when family life helped to keep growing kids on the right track? Or did we just imagine it, dream it, or wish it had been so?

There was, in fact, such a time — at least where some of us lived. We weren't rich. Our parents were not in positions of power — except with their kids — and that was enough to help keep the kids straight.

There's a story that grew up with our growing family. My sister, then a little girl, came home from Frank's Grocery Store one day with a single, forlorn-looking banana. It was dead ripe, and looked like it had come from King Tut's tomb.

Bananas were not on the grocery list she had been sent to the store to bring home, and my father demanded where she had gotten it and how. She explained that when she saw the lone banana lying on the floor beneath a bunch of bananas from which it had parted company, she picked it up, and here it was.

"And you didn't pay for it?"

"No," my sister confessed, her head down and shoulders drooped.

"Then we'll take it right back to Frank's where it belongs," my father said. And so they went, father, daughter, and one woebegone banana. When they arrived at Frank's, my father permitted his little girl to speak for herself, which — with a nervous quiver in her lower lip — she did.

Frank, feeling sorry for the child brought to justice, made gestures of compassionate protest. "That's all right, let her have the banana, Harry," he said.

"No, she took it and she has to return it to you," said my father.

In this more permissive day, this might seem like too much interference in the lives of growing children. (Kids have to explore their little worlds and express their little wishes and desires, you know — at risk of growing up into unhappy, frustrated adults.)

But this is how we learned what was expected of us. Although there has been no obvious saintliness among the Keene kids, those early influences have helped to keep us fairly straight through a lot of years since. We were expected to let what belonged to somebody else continue to belong to somebody else — unless that somebody outright gave it to us, sold it to us, or traded it for something of ours.

This code of behavior based upon parental expectation, passed from dead-ripe bananas lying on a grocery floor to how we were expected to behave in church; how to treat older people; how to be fair — the whole bag of life's experiences and relationships.

Kids are able to live up to a code of expectations when they know what the expectations are, and when these are made clear. But when they're not, kids will live down to the level of low expectations or no expectations.

Right now, teenagers — and the rest of us, with them — have a big problem. The message has gone forth, loud and clear —through TV, movies, magazines, commercials, and the pathetic misbehavior of movie stars, athletes, politicos, and other "important" people, that little or nothing above the animal level is expected of us as human beings.

Add to this the issuance of condoms in schools and clean needles on street corners — and you may as well print in bold headlines: TEENAGERS OF AMERICA: NOT TO WORRY, NOTHING IS EXPECTED OF YOU. DO WHATEVER YOU WANT, BUT BE CAREFUL DOING IT.

This low-or-no expectation message coming from the older generation to its young may be the greatest betrayal of youth ever perpetrated on the planet Earth.

Youth has always been a time of idealism and commitment, and still is despite those who would sell a whole generation cheap.

In *Emerging Trends,* published by the Princeton Religious Research Center, it was reported that a recent study revealed that 95% of teenagers believe in God, and 93% believe God loves them. Some (32%) claim they have experienced God in a personal way.

Let me ask you — does this look like a generation that should be written off for low or no expectations?

70.   A Call to Maturity

An old game has a new name — with new persons playing the same old tricks — but with new skills. The new name is "bashing." The old game is fault-finding.

It usually takes the form of blaming someone else for your own failures, mistakes, stupidity and — if you still use the word — your sins. Or you may play down your faults by playing up somebody else's. However you do it, the strategy is to make yourself look better in comparison, by making somebody else look worse.

The old game with the new name has been around a long time. The first time it was played was when Adam started bashing Eve for the fix he found himself in. And Eve, quick to learn the game, tried to make herself look faultless by blaming the serpent.

It seems we just can't live — as a nation or as individuals —without somebody or some thing to bash. It was no great surprise, when our old excuse for the fix we're in — the USSR —had its air let out, that we'd have to find a replacement.

So, conveniently, right over the horizon, there it was: Japan. There was our trouble! Not in us, but in them. We're OK; they're KO'd.

With the overheated zeal of Senator Fritz Collings of South Carolina and ten thousand other super patriots reminding Japan that we once pulvarized them with our "superiority," we're locked into a Japan-bashing spree.

And because there are so many threatened egos to defend and so many faults to cover up, the bashing game is playing itself out on hundreds of fronts. There's White House-bashing, Congress-bashing, Clinton-bashing, Brown-bashing, gray-bashing, gay-bashing.

And it doesn't stop there. There's husband-bashing, wife-bashing, job-bashing, boss-bashing. I've heard men bashing their wives, blaming them for all their failures and unfulfilled dreams. I've heard wives bashing their husbands, as though — if it were not for that male albatross hanging around their necks — they'd be supremely happy and successful — maybe even beautiful.

Bashing, by whatever name it's called, is cheap stuff, and a glaring mark of emotional immaturity. If, in the season of Lent, you want to give something up, give *it* up!

Lent is the season of human maturity — when men and women of spiritual bent make an effort to grow up and assume responsibility for their own weaknesses, failings, and their own special brand of moral aberration. You could say it is a forty-day moratorium on bashing others, and enabling us to face ourselves as our worst enemies.

The old spiritual picks up on the great theme:

> "It ain't my father, nor my mother, but it's me, O Lord,
> standin' in the need of prayer."

We trivialize the great spiritual season when we "settle" with our souls and God by denying ourselves some creature comfort or pleasure — like Hershey kisses or a dish of strawberry ice cream.

The only denial worthy of the season of Lent — and life's other seasons — is the denial of the immaturity which cannot tolerate the fact that we can be, and often are, wrong as wrong can be, and that our faults are not in our stars or in our friends or enemies, but in ourselves.

This isn't a call to self-flagellation, penetential ashes and self-defeating *mea culpas* to the rhythm of breast-beating.

It is a call to spiritual maturity which gives us the courage to accept responsibility for our own faults and, through honest confession and forgiveness, to remedy them.

All of which calls for a faith in a merciful God who knows and loves us and holds out forgiveness to the honest, repentant sinner.

Oh yes, and with the forgiveness of God, it calls for something which sometimes seems more difficult to accept —one's own forgiveness.

Bashing, fault-finding, and blaming are poisons of the soul, which are neutralized by honest-to-God confession and merciful forgiveness — from God, and from ourselves.

71.   America's Unzipped Morality

How can anybody dare to be critical of the unzipped morality of 1992 America without running the risk of being dubbed "puritanical," "Victorian," a "prude" or something worse?

The answer is there's no way to avoid the labels; they go with the territory. Unless you want to go with the flow, and passively accept everything that passes under the name of entertainment or news, or "just the way life is," you may have to stand in the corner with a booby cap on your head. In other words, you may find yourself in the company of that man whom Pontius Pilate's tough boys dressed up in funny clothes and made the target of their lewd jokes.

So, when Michael Medved, the movie critic who sees six or seven modern films a week as a reviewer, steps out from the silent, consenting crowd and speaks his mind on the sleaze that goes for motion pictures in this last decade of the 20th Century, he sets himself up for the clown makers.

And he got it, with the *Boston Globe* of August 1991 editorializing against him as a kind of puritan who wants to see every film as innocuous as "duck soup."

What Medved turns his critic pen against is the quality of the themes of some recent movies, featuring homicidal psychotic scenes, rape, and human behavior which would shame the jungle — as when Robert De Niro in a searing sex scene bites off a piece of a woman's cheek and spits it back in her mutilated face.

What sinkhole in the human soul does that come from? What sewer in the human psyche does it ooze into? What perverted appetitie does it satisfy?

Medved says, "We have enshrined ugliness as a new standard as we accept the ability to shock as a replacement for the old ability to uplift and inspire . . . the problem is a sickness of the soul."

There was the time when people went to the theater and came out feeling better about life and themselves; now they come out feeling like they ought to take a bath.

Something of those better days was revived recently when the American Film Institute honored Sidney Poitier with its annual Life Achievement Award. Poitier, modestly acknowledging the award, said it was his career-long determination to accept only those roles which lend "dignity, nobility and magnificence to human life."

Like many physical diseases, today's spiritual malaise started with a touch of naughtiness here and there, as when Rhett Butler said to Scarlett O'Hara, "Frankly, Scarlett, I don't give a damn!" Since that titillating moment, things have gradually slid from naughtiness to nausea.

And it isn't just the movies that have gone fetid; the vermin of cultural decay crawl across the TV screen. John O'Connor of the *New York Times*, a TV critic, says he's had enough of some sitcoms.

Some of the famous TV talk shows do no better. Here's a quick rundown on some of the offerings:

> Donahue: People marrying transsexuals.
> Attitudes: How an affair may help a marriage.
> Geraldo: Religious leaders and sex.
> Montel Williams: Transvestite couples.
> Maury Povich: Transsexual Tula.
> Now It Can Be Told: Washington Sex Scandals.

All of which raises the question: Why have so many good religious people been so silent so long? And why is it that some people, like Medved and O'Connor, who are not as ostensibly dedicated to making the world better, take the lead in doing what so many of us fail to do?

It's back again to the labels. We want to seem sophisticated — certainly not naive — broad-minded, tolerant, "initiated," worldly-wise. We recoil from any label that would mark us as being as "good" as we want to think we are.

Some of us would prefer to be identified with a purely secular world-view rather than to be classed with another group of people who are actually trying to make the world better —and taking all that goes with it: ridicule, caricature, thorns, and all.

What was it like for Terry Waite, the rescuer of hostages, when he himself was taken hostage — chained, blindfolded, and forced to lie in fetal position on the floor of a cell for days and nights?

What was it like when he was told he had five hours to live before the time set for his execution? And when the cold muzzle of a pistol was pressed against his head, what was that like? Most of all, how did he go through it and emerge a sane man?

This is what Barbara Walters on television program "20/20" was asking him as she sat opposite the tall, bearded Englishman, whose hostage years had clearly aged him.

The ordeal called for strength from some deep level within this man who represented the Archbishop of Canterbury in freeing other hostages before the surprising occurrence of his own captivity.

Where does such strength come from? What are its sources? This is what Barbara Walters wanted to know — what, in this interview with Waite, she was trying to elicit.

Waite shared with her some of the secrets of his survival: mental games, creating novels in his head — this sort of thing.

But this was not enough, it seemed, and Walters reached for more.

Waite made a passing reference to a Bible which he read from time to time.

"Did reading it help you?" Walters asked.

Wagging his bearded head thoughtfully, Waite said, "Not much." This was *not* the answer the interviewer obviously expected. In keeping with the heroic tradition of classical Christianity, the answer should have been, "Yes, the Bible was an ever-present source of strength and courage to me in those nights and days when all else seemed to be slipping from me."

But the brave, beautiful words did not come. Instead there was that head-wagging negative, "Not much." Waite is a deeply religious man and was pursuing a Chrisitan challenge when he fell captive.

With Waite's reputation as an honest man, the world would have believed him if he had answered Walters' question with a bold affirmative. And knowing him to be an honest man, the same people would be obliged to believe him when he said, "Not much."

Never one to give up on a line of questioning, Walters nevertheless dropped the subject immediately, as though she herself had been taken aback by the unexpected reply.

Now, what to make of this? These were the facts: a Christian man, who had suffered deeply, had survived and was capable of saying whatever he chose to say.

But the Bible — "not much" help in seeing this man through his darkest nights and starkest days? Was he saying something like this: "It's not what's in the Bible that helps you in time of need, it's what of the Bible is *in you* that is the saving grace"? Not what is printed on the gilt-edged pages, but how much of the spirit of the words has become part of you. Terry Waite had the distilled essence of the Bible within himself. He had made it part of him, and *it was there* when he needed it.

The stubborn passivity, like that of Jesus of Nazareth before Pontius Pilate. The non-violence which commanded Waite's emotions when at one time he could have gunned his way to freedom with a weapon he found in a bathroom — left there carelessly by a guard. The belief that whatever might be taken from him, his essential self, his soul, could never be taken.

This is the spirit, the very essence of the Bible, written not merely on printed pages, but upon one's innermost being. It was *there* that Terry Waite found it, and *there* it sustained him.

This may be nothing more than a lame apology for a man who may yet tell us more disturbing things about life under fire, and draw back the curtain upon what human life is like when all of the normal supports of faith and hope — and sanity — have crumbled.

We shall wait to hear from him as he reflects further upon his harrowing experience, knowing, at least, that he will speak the truth as he sees it.

73. In the Beginning

Did God "in the beginning" create "the heavens and the earth"? This question, pondered through the centuries by theologians and other believing souls, is being considered today by other minds.

It seems that a startling discovery has been made by NASA's Cosmic Background Explorer satellite in its mission to study the origins of the universe. Wispy cloud structures, millions of light years in expanse, have been discovered far out in the darkness of space.

These clouds — the largest and oldest structures in the universe, according to scientific reports — are believed to reveal how the big bang originated. Thus, it is theorized as the primordial explosion which broadcast matter throughout space — like seed falling from a man's hand — and created the universe: the stars, planets, constellations, the whole thing.

Scientists are agog over the discovery, so excited, in fact, that their usual scientific vocabulary fails them and they are rhapsodizing with words borrowed from theology and the lexicon of faith.

"It's like looking at God," said George Smoot, astrophysicist at Lawrence Berkeley Laboratory in the University of California in Berkeley.

Michael Turner, a physicist at the University of Chicago, waxed poetic: "They have found the Holy Grail of cosmology," he said.

"No less than 'the handwriting of God,'" said physicist Joel Primack of the University of California, Santa Cruz.

What has been discovered "tells us how the universe developed from an almost featureless explosion to something that's been broken up into huge clusters of galaxies and huge empty spaces," says John Mather, the satellite's chief scientist at NASA's Goddard Space Flight Center in Greenbelt, Maryland.

The scientists conjecture that before time began all of the matter of the universe was concentrated into a minute speck the size of a period at the end of a sentence.

Then, from some place, for some reason, "some unseen, immeasurable force," to quote an unnamed British scientist, caused the tiny dot of highly concentrated matter to reach trillions of degrees, then explode, sending bits and pieces on an endlessly expanding course throughout space.

So, what we know — or think we know — has led us once again into the depths of mystery; and, like children, we are left nearly speechless, except for those words that speak of God.

Those who don't believe in a creative force which made the first move may be nudged to reconsider their position. And those who believe in God may be obliged to reconsider their belief system, and allow for the possibility that God is greater by infinity than they have ever conceived God to be.

From this point on, there's no place for smug disbelief — or smug belief. Clearly, smugness, the unbelieving kind and the believing kind, has been blasted to bits by that "big bang" with which everything began.

Those who say that the idea of God is a refuge for weak minds and childish emotions may find such thinking a bit difficult to maintain in the presence of scientists, physicists, and astrophysicists who seem unable, right now, to speak a sentence that doesn't have "God" in it.

And those who believe in God will not be able to afford the luxury of sitting down after Sunday dinner, discoursing blandly about God as though they carried the Almighty in their back pocket.

We may all find it proper to be willing to sit down before the mystery as children and be prepared to alter our faith to make it less parochial in an ever-expanding universe shrouded in mystery.

Indeed it could be that atheism and theism, science and religion — sobered by mystery — may come closer together, as some of the cocksureness of all of us is reduced to appropriate humility in the presence of something which no human mind is able to explain — or explain away.

74. Let's Make a Heaven of Earth

What on earth is happening in heaven? What under heaven is happening on Earth?

Three figures in white (not angels, at least as we think of angels) stood recently in triangular formation on a space vehicle called Endeavor, traveling at a speed of 17,000 miles per hour, and "captured" a communications satellite moving at the same speed, drew it inside the bay of the space shuttle, repaired it, clamped a booster rocket onto it, and launched it into space to follow the orbit originally planned for it.

All that's happening "up there" — up where we look when we speak of God and heaven and angels. As someone quipped, "They've made a garage of heaven."

Let's just say heaven's not what it used to be — or what we thought it was. In addition to satellites orbiting the Earth and an abandoned automobile resting on the moon with its tire tracks rutting the moon dust, there are meteors, chunks of rock, zipping here and there through the heavenly spaces. Rocks in heaven!

With heaven different from what it used to be, where can we center our tender thoughts, our hopes and dreams, and longings?

Well, there's Earth, that beautiful little planet with its veil of clouds spinning beneath the space shuttle where the men in white work. Viewed from up there, Earth is seen with new eyes. Out beyond the orbit of the Endeavor, there are planets, lifeless as the moon. No bird songs in the morning, no sweet "good nights," no boy-meets-girl, no kisses, no embraces, no fond plans, no dreams, no children's voices.

But back there — or "up" there, however it may seem when you're in space, floating weightlessly, not knowing up from down, there's that marvel of marvels — a planet teeming with dear life, people falling in love, marrying, little babies being born, seedtime and harvest replenishing furrowed fields, clouds gathering, dropping their moisture upon dry acres, greening them with life.

Now *there's* a real discovery — a place with all the possibilities that the heaven of our dreams is made of: peace, love, joy.

Here and there on earth are little enclaves where the best of our heavenly dreams are reality. But there is something else, something dark and ominous: Human beings clawing and tearing at one another, bodies lying in stark uncaring streets, the bloody harvest of hatred.

Heaven is a longing, something for later on. But heaven can wait while we do our own thing on Earth. In "the sweet by and by," heaven will come. In the meantime, let us have our own wills, our own egoistic ways. Get what we can, as much as we can, from whomever we can — cheat, rob, rape, plunder, kill.

Some perversions of the Christian religion have encouraged human beings to subdue the Earth, lay waste its resources, treat fellow human beings — especially those who are "different from us" — as inferior, put here for our purposes, to be thrown away like disposable cups when we've finished with them.

Christianity, the "saving" religion, needs itself to be saved from some of its most ardent followers — saved in the name of that man who "came and dwelt among us," who said, "Inasmuch as you did it to one of the least of these, my brethren, you did it to me."

Authentic Christianity is not so much heaven-centered as it is Earth-centered. It's not angel-centered, it's man-centered. The God of the Christian faith is Earth-oriented, human-oriented, caring infinitely what happens here on this little planet spinning, like a boy's top, around the sun.

Maybe heaven can wait, but Earth can't. It's too fragile, its people too much in need of God's love expressed through other human beings.

The streets of Los Angeles, where riots and plundering laid waste hundreds of buildings and killed or maimed scores of human beings, cry out "for the sons of God to be revealed" —men and women who pray and live the words their Master taught them: "Thy kingdom come, they will be done on Earth . . ."

God, our Grandfather . . . our Mother and Father . . . our Mother . . . our Lover. . .

If this hits you like a dash of ice water down your back, there will be some who will sympathize with you, but some others will look at you and wonder why you're shivering.

These words of address to God were adopted at the United Methodist General Conference as acceptable modes of reference to diety.

The vote for adoption of the denomination's *Book of Worship* (809-149), which includes the new language, was greeted enthusiastically, and given a standing ovation by the nearly 1,000 delegates meeting in Louisville, Kentucky from May 5 to 15, 1992.

This worship resource, while including the traditional words of reference and address to God, embraces the new language, a legacy to present and future generations.

If it is a legacy of enrichment of the language of faith and devotion — as some parts of the *Book of Worship* undoubtedly are — this is good. Perhaps the time has come for some of the ancient forms to be supplemented by terms and concepts more in harmony with 20th century thinking.

The faith inherited from the past has been indicted as being weighted in favor of masculine pride and prerogative, originating as it did in a time when women were considered inferior to men. Contemporary feminism has succeeded in correcting this historic imbalance, with women now serving in important ecclesiastical positions, including pastors, district superintendents, and bishops. But God — Mother?

And with people living longer — into the seventies and eighties — there is an increased appreciation of the relationship of youth with age. Grandparents are important, and many people in their thirties and forties speak of a grandmother or grandfather as one of the sources of warmth, affection, and inspiration in their growing years. But God — Grandfather?

Along with the positive images evoked by the word, there are other pictures not so positive: an old man with flowing white hair and beard; someone who is not up to the latest in TVs, VCRs, computers, Fax machines and the like; a senior citizen who has hung it up, retired, a dropout in life's parade; nice and all that —maybe a little indulgent of younger people, but somewhat doddering, uncertain, dim of vision and hard of hearing, and perhaps even a little bit befogged, a nice guy and all that — but God?

With the modern world's thirst for love, the soul and body's need to love and be loved, and with sex becoming the shorthand for love between and among the genders, the cry for love is poignant. But God — lover?

The word links up with synonyms and images far from flattering to God: Casanova, Don Juan, Romeo, philanderer, ladies' man, someone engaged in extramarital activities.

These less savory associations of the word are not exclusively modern. In both the Old and New Testament, "lover" bears shady, even shabby, connotations.

The intention of the *Book of Worship* is clear, even commendable, up to a point. Such intention is to create an image of the divine that is approachable, warm, understanding, and responsive to the deepest human longings.

But there is a point beyond which this trend should not go! Such point is where the re-imaging robs the concept of God of its moral fiber.

The God of the Bible is the source and guarantor of moral law as well as love, who blesses those who abide by the laws governing human life and relationships, and chastens those who do not abide by them — often letting the offenders suffer the consequences of their offenses until they repent and seek forgiveness and reconciliation.

Perhaps we need to be careful how we attempt to improve upon the one image of God which embraces both love and discipline: Father.

Remember the jingle "Who takes care of the caretaker's daughter while the caretaker's out taking care"?

Give it a little twist: Who takes care of the soul-saver's soul while the soul-saver's out saving souls?

A news release in the *National and International Religion Report* of April 20, 1992, states: "A majority of American pastors are suffering from spiritual burnout, many are buckling under family and financial pressures, and a large percentage have considered quitting the ministry."

H. B. London, Jr., a clergyman and director of the Pastoral Ministries Department of Focus on the Family, concluded from a study involving 500 ministers that pastors "are living an unbalanced life."

Seldom do spiritual leaders have anyone with whom they can talk about their own spiritual needs and personal problems without running the risk of sabotaging their professional careers.

What parishioner wants to subject himself to the disturbing experience of listening to his pastor confess his sins and transgressions?

What member of the clergy is prepared to risk baring his or her soul to a fellow pastor, much less to a church superior who keeps a little black book, and may jot down a note or two as a reminder that Jim or Joan (ministers come in both genders these days) is less than the best candidate for the next promotion? From such a soul-baring on, the minister is considered "damaged goods" to be sold at a discount price.

Yet there is something about the very nature of the profession which pulls, pushes, squeezes, and crunches a pastor —often to the breaking point.

In a recent meeting of clergy and their spouses, dealing with the stresses placed upon the profession, one of the fellow clergy counted one fourth of those present who are either divorced or considering divorce.

Depression, the mental and emotional illness which afflicts large numbers of the American population, is not unknown among the clergy. Sexual promiscuity and marital infidelity, once a secret matter hid behind the closed doors of parsonages, are now shouted from parsonage house tops.

The role of clergy in American society has long been a hallowed one. The professional minister, while being like other human beings — "a little lower than the angels" — has been considered somewhat more angel than human. And many clergy gladly buy into this fancy for reasons best known to themselves.

Yet, as human as he or she is, no amount of flattery or self-adulation ought to be permitted to deny this fact. It's when a clergyman forgets or denies his human status that he is close to a fall.

Add to this the fact that the position of clergy is that of one set apart, looked up to as a spiritual guide and moral mentor. This is potent, heady stuff — an intoxicating mixture which can easily destabilize a clergyman or any other human being.

One of the sources of clergy problems is inadequate salary. The pastor is expected to maintain a good appearance, keep a good car, and take care of spouse and children, often on a salary which barely provides for the expenses incurred in "keeping up appearances."

Of the 500 clergy polled by London in his study, 90% of them admitted that they had been discouraged in the preceding three months, and 70% of these confessed they had debated whether they should remain in the ministry.

Talk with a member of the clergy about these matters, and the pastor's natural diffidence and conditioned professional modesty, coupled with an understandable desire to avoid an embarrassing subject, may incline him or her to deny having such problems.

But scratch the professional facade deep enough, and you will find a human being who wants — or at one time wanted —with heart, soul, mind and strength to serve God and help others in their hours of need, who himself or herself needs help.

77. Easy Answers to Hard Questions

Joseph Bishop, a little three-and-a-half-year-old boy, visiting his father in Yucca Valley in Southern California, was crushed to death by a falling chimney which collapsed when an earthquake rumbled through the valley recently.

In a world where many people want to believe in a good and merciful God, hard questions surface: Why earthquakes that demolish homes and injure people? And in the name of God, why should this little boy have been the only fatality, this innocent child who had just begun to live?

For hard questions there are always those who offer easy answers like: "It was because God needed a little angel in heaven and so took him." How often has this well-meaning but empty-headed bromide been given to broken-hearted parents after the death of a child?

What warped impression of God must such a palliative leave in the minds of bereaved parents? If God needs more angels, it's probably not in heaven where all souls are safe in the Everlasting Arms, but here on Earth, where human beings struggle and sweat and curse and kill.

If God wanted an angel in heaven, why go about it this way? Most anybody could think of a better way than letting a chimney fall on a little kid.

Then there's Sidney Reso, the Exxon executive kidnapped from his own driveway in North Jersey, held for a ransom of eighteen and a half million dollars, and subjected to abuse which ended his life. His decomposed body was found buried in a remote spot infested with ticks and tangled with underbrush.

Why does God permit such things to happen? Again, there's always the easy answer: "Well, you see, my friend, God created human beings with free will, and this dear man's abductors were free to do whatever they chose to do. For God to deprive us of free will would make puppets of us all."

Well, let Irene Seale and her husband Arthur Seale, the alleged abductors, keep their free will, but couldn't God, without spoiling some great plan, have directed their free will to other alternatives which would have left Sidney Reso alive and free to go to his job and return to his family at day's end?

Another "defender of the faith" might say, "Some good will come out of it, you'll see. God wouldn't let a thing like this happen otherwise."

No doubt in the long run something good will emerge from all the evil happenings of this world, but will the good be a better good than the good that might have come if the evil had not occurred?

Others with easy answers to hard questions might say, "Well, he must have been a bad man despite appearances otherwise. God wouldn't have permitted this to happen to a really good man."

This is the thesis advanced by Job's "comforters." In case you haven't heard of Job, he's an Old Testament character whose happy and prosperous existence suddenly fell apart. His friends told him he must have done something bad sometime, or God would not have allowed such devastation to befall him. Quite understandably, Job did not appreciate his friends' helpfulness.

The answer that came to Job in his nightmarish bottom-of-the-pit experience came in the form of a series of questions from God, beginning with "Where were you when I laid the foundation of the Earth?"

Each question led into deeper mystery, until the mind of Job foundered. His one question, as to why a good man should suffer, was lost in a sea of mystery.

The big question is why is there anything at all? Why should we be born? Why, after so many years of non-being, should we suddenly come into being, emerge — then take our exit?

The great answer to the great question is mystery. Life, from beginnng to end, is a mystery, embraced in mystery. And if we had not let ourselves become so cozily familiar with the idea of God that we think God should report to us on everything, we would bow in silence before the mystery. This could be our purest reverence, our most devout worship.

I'm glad I was born. Oh, there have been a few times when I might not have said that with gusto or pure delight, but those times blew over and the old gladness returned.

Since that day in October, longer ago than I can believe, there have been some bad times as well as good, but through it all there has been a real *joie de vivre,* a genuine appreciation of the supreme privilege of living.

To be alive, to see, to feel, to breathe, to hope, to love — this has to be the greatest thing God ever thought of and translated into reality.

I have the feeling that my parents, those two young people in their late twenties, couldn't really afford me — one more mouth to feed, another body to clothe and keep warm in winter, and doctors' bills to pay.

Furthermore, they already had the "ideal family" — a boy and a girl. Anything after that was bound to be redundant. Not that they thought this way, though if they had, they wouldn't have been the first or the last.

But, being the parents they were, believing in God and life, once my life began, they more or less accepted me — or what I now call me. Actually, at the time, I was nothing more than a small group of cells multiplying at a rapid rate in the cradle of my mother's womb — my first water bed.

My young parents weren't up on all of the now-familiar concepts about fetal tissue, first trimester, second trimester, amniocentesis, and the like. They just knew that a new life was stirring down in the liquid darkness, and they were willing — or at least not unwilling — to have that life continue and emerge at last to see the bright, glad light of day.

I'm sure they could have done something to throw a monkey wrench into the machinery of life, and put an end to it. Then my mother could have become un-pregnant. They could then have continued as a family of four. They could live happily ever after, with only a dimming memory of a once unfortunate episode in their lives. Such things were heard of and talked about in our neighborhood.

The young couple, my parents, cuddling close on a cold night in January, with the winter wind sighing down the chimney, had their brief moment of pleasure, though the pleasure must have faded quickly when the little unnamed growing life that was me, (I choose to be ungrammatical at this point) began to stir and then kick. Happily, I gave them their moment of pleasure on a freezing night.

I tried hard to give them pleasure after I emerged, but I'm not sure it ever really made up for the inconvenience, discomfort, expense, and pain — but they seemed happy with my efforts.

Although they were young, they were old-fashioned young, and had some good old-fashioned ideas like life is from God, and therefore sacred. Hence, don't kick it out of the one place where God intended it should be secure and comfortable.

This little excursion into intimate autography is not meant to celebrate one individual's personal life, but to celebrate life itself. Whether to let live or not let live are questions set in a burning focus in 20th-century America. For reasons often no more justifiable than inconvenience, discomfort, and expense, human life in its most helpless beginnings is being terminated with every sunrise, sunset, and high noon.

The numbers are heartbreaking. An honest look at one human life vacuumed violently from its mother's womb is enough to make a strong man weep and head for the nearest men's room to throw up.

This leads to the inescapable conclusion that if thinking, feeling human beings knew what they were doing — knew the whole truth about abortion — they would give it long, serious consideration, and cringe at the thought.

The silent cry of the crucified unborn rises above their Calvary and mingles with that other cry from a cross: "Father, forgive them, for they know not what they do."

 # Beyond the Absurd

The recent U. S. Supreme Court decision disallowing prayer in public high school graduation ceremonies rocked the nation and almost half of the Court itself.

Four of the nine justices — including Chief Justice William Rhenquist, Justices Byron R. White, Clarence Thomas, and Anton Scalia — opined that the decision and the twisted logic behind it was "beyond the absurd."

The Founding Fathers whom we refer to in almost reverential terms would have been at least ruffled and perhaps humiliated by what some of our *floundering fathers* have made of the Constitution.

The First Amendment reads: "Congress shall make no law respecting an establishment of religion, or prohibiting the free exercise thereof; or abridging the freedom of speech."

In this case (Lee v. Weisman, June 24, 1992) the Court engaged in a process which the Constitution denies to Congress — disavowing the right of an establishment of religion to express itself through its ordained representative — in this instance a Jewish rabbi — in a peaceful public gathering.

Since prayer is one of the traditional exercises of religion, the Court's decision is nothing less than a renunciation of that clause in the First Amendment.

Beyond that, the decision is an abridgement of free speech, since prayer is speech in its loftiest form.

Does it strike you as strange that the Supreme Court has zealously upheld the right of free speech, even to the point of permitting stomach-turning pornography, yet can't seem to find reasons under the freedom-of-speech clause to allow prayer at graduation ceremonies?

Justice Kennedy's argument runs: "The First Amendment's religious clauses mean that religious beliefs and religious expressions are too precious to be either proscribed or prescribed by the State."

Is the good justice suggesting that religion is such a precious thing that it ought to be kept under lock and key, away from all that might sully it — or be influenced by it?

Painfully, this seems to be the direction in which his thinking heads when he says, "the design of the Constitution is that preservation and transmission of religious beliefs and worship is a responsibility and choice committed to the private sphere . . ."

Does this mean that God and religion are to be "privatized," marginalized, elbowed off into some obscure corner reserved for the irrelevant, a limbo for cast-off things that just don't matter?

Government and what is touched by government represents an area of vital concern to the American people. If religion is pushed out of every place where the long shadow of government falls, how can anybody be expected to take religion seriously?

The majority opinion, written by Justice Kennedy, says, "high school graduation is one of life's most significant occasions, and a student is not free to absent herself from the exercise . . . it is therefore unconstitutional to permit prayer as part of the significant occasion."

What a case of turning logic on its head! It would seem to most people, I dare say, that just because graduation is such a significant occasion in a young person's life, the opportunity to lift the occasion to its highest level of significance through the acknowledgement of God should never be denied.

Another point made in the majority argument stated that, "since adolescents are often susceptible to peer pressure . . . the state may no more use social pressure to enforce orthodoxy than it may use direct means."

So they admit the reality of peer pressure which more often than not pushes human behavior down into the slime, but will not dare even to appear to support peer pressure that lifts life toward the stars.

I heartily agree with Justice Scalia that much of this majority opinion's thinking is "beyond the absurd."

80.   The Baby Boomer Breakaway

There's something demeaning in the generational designation "baby boomer." It suggests a generation of grown-ups toddling around in diapers, waiting for their milk and Pablum to be served by an older generation.

The picture may be more factual than caricature — not in the way "baby boomers" view themselves, but in the way the older generation sees them.

To the consternation of the bearers of religious tradition and custom, these thirty-something people are turning away from their inherited religious faiths like babies refusing the bottle and nipple before having passed the suckling age.

A recent study by the Lilly Foundation reveals that, although they were brought up in the faith of their fathers and mothers, great numbers of them — reared in what are called the mainline churches — declare they will never attend church again.

The church elders — clergy, leading lay people, and others —are shocked and wounded by the breakaway attitudes of their children in the faith. Studies are under way to attempt to determine the causes of the alienation.

It seems these 30-to 40-year-olds are just not satisfied to live on the cliches and platitudes of a predigested faith, however sacred it may be to their elders. It's not that they aren't religious; they are. It's not that they don't have or want a faith to live by; they do. But they want a faith they have to bite off, chew up, and digest — even if they get indigestion in the process.

One of the researchers said, "The church just doesn't 'do' anything for them." Another member of the research team said this generation is striving to understand how the older generation can accept the current level of evil, suffering, and injustice without great efforts to improve. But the boomers find little help in the mainline churches.

This silent rebellion against the traditional mainline churches — Methodist, Presbyterian, Episcopal, and Baptist — is partially rooted in the feeling that some of the churches have absorbed the values of 20th-century American culture, including sexual permissiveness, self-centered aims, and a materialistic view of life.

In other words, the church — as seen by the thirty-something people — is nothing more than a continuer of "things as they are." Therefore, it applies its expressed or implied blessing to whatever is "in" for the sake of seeming contemporary but inoffensive to the prevailing culture.

An honest, penetrating look at the mainline churches may reveal that some have long gone with the flow, blessing wars, sanctifying greed, fawning over the rich and influential. They may have won the reputation of being "mainline" because they have fallen in with the styles and mores around them, instead of questioning and challenging them.

The baby boomers, born in the midst of wars, and growing up in a recession, may want a totally different experience of worship and faith, sharing the deepest levels of their psyches with one another. Then, juxtiposed into certain situations, they can sit down and unabashedly express their deepest faiths and gravest doubts. There they can discuss the meaning of life honestly, openly, and without feeling the constraint to resort to the tired cliches they have received from the past — bromides calculated to tranquilize the inquiring mind as it presses against the boundaries of thought and feeling.

It may be that the baby boomers are discouraged with some of the mainline churches because they seldom hear from the pulpits any prophetic pronouncements addressed to the evils which alienate people from one another — from their own souls — and from God.

They would no doubt appreciate hearing a prophetic voice like that of Archbishop George Carey, the titular head of the Church of England, inveighing against the propertied and privileged persons ensconced in the lap of luxury while millions of their countrymen are out of work and thousands of mortgages are being forclosed by some of these same priviliged people — some of whom may have been sitting before the Archbishop as he preached.

Whatever has caused the exodus of the baby boomers, it means that serious thinking, and drastic changes, must be undertaken in complacent mainline churches.

81.   Prostitution of the Sacred

If there's anything more spiritually devastating than the denial of God, it's pious God-talk marinated in the juices of political emotions.

When God is reduced to a buzz word to get political banners waving and the party faithful marching in lock step to the tune of some political piper, sensitive stomachs begin to turn.

Presidential candidate George Bush dispensed God language as if he possessed a copyright on the sacred words. In a recent speech he roundly berated the opposition because the word GOD, which he spelled out letter by letter, did not appear in their platform.

The President is no doubt a good man and a religious man; however, he is also a politician who knows the powerful appeal which sacred references have among many voters. But he appears to be using the great reconciling name to divide and conquer.

Many in his own party are offended. Jack Kemp recently expressed the hope that the presidential campaign would not become a religious war, a jihad, dividing the country into "true believers" and "infidels."

There are people in both parties who believe in God as much as the President does — who, in fact, believe so deeply that they would not prostitute the divine name for any political advantage. These people resent the shameless politicization of the sacred.

Talk about the Judeo-Christian tradition is falling through the political atmosphere like confetti and red, white, and blue balloons at the recent party conventions.

This great tradition of political party conventions has been with us a long time and is a vital part of the American experience. It has as its centerpiece such profound reverence for God that in the beginning the divine name was barely spoken for fear of sullying it with the stain of the human tongue.

The use of God language and religious symbols to call attention to one's self for political, social, financial, or any other self-serving purpose is a violation of the great tradition which some are blatantly ballyhooing and hawking like a political gimcrack.

There's a quote from *The Interpreter's Bible* which seems to fit the huckstering of religious values for rallying the troops: "The cheap and easy use of the divine name to cover up poverty of thought and feeling."

A further quote from the same source on the same theme: "Religion for many people consists in the good feeling aroused by the repetition of certain words — or phrases. This type of piety can be recognized by its extreme harshness in the denunciation of those who do not use them."

This kind of violation of the sacred is an offense against those who embrace religious values in their own sincere and modest ways, and it drives a wedge through American society — further dividing a nation which is already divided and needs the healing that can come from religion.

In the name of God, let politicians and hangers-on of all parties respect the great Judeo-Christian tradition enough to avoid using it to claim divine sponsorship for all the hubris, egotism, and just plain meanness which parade under all political banners.

And let's avoid the Pharisee-like posturing of those who stand in public places and boast, "I thank ... God that I am not as other men are, extortioners, unjust, adulterers."

Only one who hasn't explored the shadowy depths of his own soul, or who thinks God is a fool, could stand before God and pose as lily white, unblemished, and unstained.

The pseudo-righteous, like the Pharisee praying his self-praising prayer in the temple, were the ones who crucified the best man who ever lived. And that was because he dared to kick the lid off their garbage can, and they didn't like the bad odor.

If we can't use religion to heal the alienation and wounds in society and in our own souls, it might be better to keep silent on the subject until we're ready for the better use of religion, which is love.

82. When the Saints Come Marching In

Sainthood is not what you'd call a top drawer priority on the agenda of most 20th-century Americans.

Even "good" people who go to church regularly, say their prayers, read their Bibles, and celebrate Christmas and Easter would frankly confess, "We're no saints."

Is this smiling disavowal of a noble standard of human living an admission that we're "not that good," and in all honesty we don't want to be?

If so, we may be missing an opportunity to inject into the organism of American life a powerful stimulant which could produce more genuine results than all the political speeches and fiscal proposals that have ever been made.

This is what George H. Gallup, Jr., the eminent researcher, seems to be suggesting in his new book, *The Saints Among Us*, which he co-authored with Timothy Jones.

In a survey which is the basis for the book, Gallup tested the waters of contemporary America for signs of unannounced and uncelebrated saintliness among 1,052 Americans.

He discovered what he no doubt suspected was true —that throughout the country there are ordinary workaday Americans who manifest in their beliefs and daily behavior the unmistakable marks of saintliness. They're not self-conscious saints concerned about the tilt and glitter of their halos; they're just honest-to-goodness good people, *the salt of the Earth.*

Gallup's saints are people who have made a deep and abiding commitment of their time, talent, abilities, possessions, and their lives to God.

They are individuals whose "journey inward" is balanced by their "journey outward" — reaching out to their fellow human beings in need.

They are gracious, unprejudiced persons who would welcome a family of a different race as their next-door neighbors.

They are happily fulfilled men and women. They are people who forgive but don't forget. They remember their own faults and offenses and never forget them, but lift them daily into the light of the forgiveness of God. They forgive because they don't forget how they have been wounded by others. They remember the offenses and realize that others like themselves have often offended in ignorance, frustration, or jealousy. They know that just to be alive is sometimes an offense to someone. In other words, they have so thoroughly immersed themselves in the human condition that they are fully initiated human beings. And they have so immersed themselves in the grace of God that they forgive others and themselves as God forgives.

These are saints in everyday clothes. I know a number of people personally who, though they would not presume to consider themselves unusually good, and might even be embarrassed by the mere suggestion, are — in Gallup's terms — definitely to be counted among the saints.

"We're all searching for goodness," says Gallup. "We long for it . . . Such goodness is available to all through the inspiration of the saints. The power of their lives is felt to an extraordinary degree."

Gallup feels that most churches don't do enough to cultivate saints. The concept seems to have slipped through the cracks in ecclesiastical structures.

More time, money, and energy are spent on loftier church steeples, lovelier stained-glass windows, more gracious church parlors, and well-equipped church kitchens than in trying to make people good — much less, saintly.

Gallup and his co-author Timothy Jones feel that, for some people, "saintliness may seem out of step with a world where ozone holes, ICBM missiles, and 'crack' babies call for hard-hitting pragmatism."

But both men agree that there may not be a more realistic pragmatism for this world than the blessed pragmatism of the saints.

The co-authors see the way of the saints as a viable alternative lifestyle, standing in sharp contrast to an obviously failed ego-centered way of life which has produced harvests of blood, burning, and blight.

There are thousands of Americans claiming their right to "the pursuit of happiness," but never quite finding what they pursue. For these persons there may be no better way than the way the saints have found: the displacement of EGO by GOD, getting by giving, fear by faith, despair by hope, indifference and hate by love.

This could be the best time in the world for the saints to come marching in.

83.   Into All the World

Something's happening out there. Religion is breaking out of the little boxes where it has been held hostage.

There's a whole big world beyond the stained-glass windows, Gothic arches, and the redolence of burning candles. Religion has an affinity for that world.

As it breaks out of the stifling atmosphere of musty antiquity and sclerotic formality, it breathes more deeply, flexes its muscles, and stands taller.

Take what's happening in southern Florida, for example. Many church buildings, like houses, have gone with the wind of Hurricane Andrew, and people are reaching out to people. Many families who have lost their homes are asking for Bibles and spiritual help in dealing with their devastated lives.

"I think God's calling his church out from behind the walls," said Tony Poncetti, who is a member of the Miami Baptist Association's relief team.

Franklin Beam, an associate director of MBA, said the storm might be considered an answer to prayer. "We did not pray for Hurricane Andrew, but what we did pray for was for God to open the door to let the people of Miami know that Jesus loves them and we love them too."

Church groups across the country, including many in Delaware and Maryland, have delivered truckloads of relief supplies to the stricken areas.

Miami pastors who have been praying together and joining forces to break down racial barriers are saying that the post-hurricane cleanup is helping to promote unity. "Right now," says Scott Nyborg, director of Latin American Mission's Christ for the City campaign in Miami, it doesn't matter who's working with whom." Their campaign We Are One has brought black, white, Haitian, and Hispanic pastors together.

Now take a look across the country to Los Angeles. At CBS in Television City on Fairfax Street, Jack Hart who is art director of "The Price Is Right" and "Family Feud," two popular TV shows, is the leader of a weekly lunchtime Bible study group.

Charles Kappelman, an active member of the United Methodist Church, was one of the pioneers of the group. He's still an active participant. The group experienced a groundswell of renewed interest when Irwin Barnett, a production supervisor of "The Price Is Right," was converted several years ago. Barnett, once a gay activist, began affirming his newfound faith to his coworkers and urged them to join the Bible study group.

Now to Washington, where the Redskins have been dubbed "the most religious" team in the National Football League. More than half the men on Joe Gibbs' squad seriously consider themselves born-again Christians.

Heads that meet in a huddle on the playing field meet again in another kind of huddle — weekly meetings for Bible studies. Among them are Charles Mann, Darrell Green, Art Monk, and Monte Coleman. Running back Ernest Byner told *Washingtonian* magazine that he was baptized two years ago in Darrell Green's Jacuzzi. "There's a great spirit of Christ on this team. Coach Gibbs' openness to the gospel invited this atmosphere," says defensive lineman Tim Johnson.

Meanwhile on campus, college students who are members of campus-centered groups are reported to be healthier and happier than students who have no such affiliation. This was brought to light in a study by University of Western Ontario sociologists Gail Grankel and Ted Hewitt. A conclusion of the report is that the more "religious" a student is — in terms of the experience of God's presence, biblical knowledge, and the practice of prayer — the better off he or she is. These students are judged to be significantly healthier physically and psychologically.

So church doors are opening outward, stained-glass

windows are being raised. The church is at last following the words of its Master, "Go into all the world . . ."

84.   Behold the Man

Is violence innate in the human male? Or is it the result of male inability or unwillingness to face and deal honestly with feelings and experiences common to all human beings, men and women alike?

Is male independence and emotional remoteness — the kind of thing which kills tenderness in men's relationships with women and children and other men — an inborn quality? Or does it come from fear of being hurt or found lacking in traditional masculinity?

Questions like these were posed at a convention of the American Psychological Association in Washington, D.C. recently, where Ron Levant of the Harvard Medical School and editor of *The Journal of Family Psychology* riveted the attention of 17,000 professionals as he discussed what it means to be a man in the modern world.

"The code of masculinity has collapsed," said Levant. "To many men, particularly midlife men, the question of what it means to be a man today is one of the most persistent issues in their lives."

Not so long ago Levant was a voice crying in the wilderness when he talked about these matters. According to an article by Dianne Aprile in the *Louisiana Courier-Journal,* when Levant and a few colleagues started workshops and seminars about "a new psychology" of men, only seven people showed up — "six of them women, and the other a man wearing long hair pulled back in a ponytail . . ."

From seven to 17,000! Voices crying in the wilderness of rape, mugging, murder — for a different kind of masculinity in a world grown sick of the old kind.

This means there's a search on for a paradigm, a model, a hero. Someone to point to and say, "That's it; that's what it means to be a man!"

At this point in the script there ought to be the note: "Enter Jesus of Nazareth." Not exactly a John Wayne or a Rambo, but certainly not a Casper Milquetoast either.

Here's a man in whose nature there was a fine balance of strength and tenderness, intelligence and emotion, a man focused but not lacking peripheral vision, assertive but not overbearing, self-confident but not cocky, accepting but not undifferentiating.

"Ecce Homo!" said Pontius Pilate with a studied official gesture, introducing Jesus of Nazareth to the crowd intent upon his crucifixion. "Behold the man!" Those words have taken on a larger meaning than the Roman politico could have imagined. Not just a man or even the man caught in the light of a historic situation, but man, the flesh-and-blood idea of what a man was intended to be. Not rapacious, but healing, not self-serving, but serving others, not any man's enemy, but every man's truest friend.

The record of his few short years offers glimpses of him in action. Standing with a little child cradled in his arms, whispering half to the child and half to those standing by, listening, "of such is the Kingdom of Heaven." Many a politician running for office, eager to impress his constituents, has re-played that scene. It's good to know where they got it.

Another scene: A young woman, "taken in adultery," cringes before a crowd of men who have taken it upon themselves to stone her to death for her sin. Positioning himself between the woman and the would-be executioners, Jesus says, "Let him who is without sin cast the first stone." One by one the men back off.

Respect for life, compassion for the wounded, the courage to stand up and be counted when this could lead to being killed. These were the qualities present in that man. It is safe to say that most every man in his better moments would like to be like that man from Nazareth.

For nearly 2,000 years he has stood before us, praised, worshipped, and "defended" in a thousand battles by men whose manhood had totally not reached the depth of his. The one thing we have not done in his name is to accept him — if not as Lord, at least as the ultimate man, the man psychologists like

Harvard's Levant and people throughout the world are looking for.

In our search for the meaning of human life, perhaps we have looked too long into the ooze and slime, too long into the caves and crannies, listened too long to unintelligible growls and grunts, and have not been tuned into that one sane voice in a mad world.

Index

169

Continued on next page.

Continued on next column.

Continued on next page.

Continued on next page.